Throw Away Your Visi

What others are s

Throw Away Your Vision Board...

"Dr. Farber has done it again! Neil has created several compelling reads guiding thousands to positive thinking and success through change in behavior and outlook. Throw Away Your Vision Board is his most provocative work to date and I would encourage anyone who has a desire for success to read this book. As a person of action, I believe this manuscript has the potential to truly revolutionize how people positively plan for the path to success."

-- **Dr. Joseph Kerschner, Dean and Executive Vice President, Medical College of Wisconsin, Professor of Otolaryngology and Communication Sciences.**

"If you are reading this endorsement you have taken action to look at this book, congratulations on your first step in truly learning "The Secret". Dr. Farber shares a well informed and research based approach to validating why "action" is crucial to being able to create the word "attraction". This latest book is a motivational work that stimulates enough insightful controversy to help upgrade your "vision board" into an "action board" so you will actually achieve what you desire versus dreaming about what you want."

-- **Mark S. Gridley, MBA, FACHE, Executive Vice President, Chief Operating Officer, FHN Regional Healthcare**

Neil E. Farber, MD, PhD

"Outstanding book! Dr. Farber, a highly accomplished physician, scientist, author, life coach, and martial artist, deftly and thoroughly dismantles the concept of vision boarding, replacing it with a powerful, science-based approach appropriately called Action Boarding. To achieve more, of course having a vision helps but it's the action that flows from a solid foundation in one's personal principles and core beliefs about themselves and their world that gets the job done! Farber's command of this topic is encyclopedic and his writing is direct, convincing, and hugely entertaining. I read this book in a single sitting, completely losing track of time!"

- **Peter Bandettini, PhD. Chief, Section on Functional Imaging Methods, Director, Functional MRI Core Facility, National Institute of Mental Health, Editor-in-Chief of the Journal *NeuroImage*.**

"Throw away your vision board...or use it for kindling. With hard work and very strong determination, I have had great personal success as a world champion martial artist, sculptor, marathon runner, gymnast, architect, artist, musician, inventor, film producer, and editor. None of my achievements were accomplished by vision boarding or wishing for help from the universe. As Farber writes, you are in control of your journey. Your first step on the journey to success is to read this book and follow Dr. Farber's Key to Achieve Principles!

--**Maurice Elmalem, PhD, 7-Time World Martial Arts Champion, 8-Time Guinness Worlds Record Holder, 10th Dan Black Belt and Editor of *Budo* Magazine, Who's Who in Architectural Design.**

Throw Away Your Vision Board

"Farber enthusiastically encourages us to throw away our vision boards and effectively argues that accomplishment is a function of process visualization, gratitude, mindfulness, accountability, positivity and action. Farber offers us an intuitive and accessible alternative, integrating those principles into a toolbox that best enables achievement."

- Dr. Michael Roizen, Physician, Chief Wellness Officer & Institute Chair at Cleveland Clinic, Chief Medical Consultant to the Dr. Oz show, 4-time NY Times Bestselling Author of the YOU series.

"Dr. Neil Farber has penned an inspiring and insightful battle plan for anyone who is serious about achieving a life goal. He clarifies the folly of utilizing a Vision Board and relying on the Law of Attraction to reach these goals. After reading this book, you will understand why you need to throw away your Vision Board and employ a truly effective Action Board. Full of interesting historical references, scientific facts and trivia, and loaded with common sense, Dr. Farber's work will allow you to focus and redirect your energy toward any desired accomplishment. Throughout our lifetimes, we all hope, wish, even believe wonderful things will happen to us. Instead of living in the fantasy world of a Vision Board, follow the recommendations in these pages to take action. Make your life happen. This book provides the blueprint to set you on your way."

Dr. Gregg Moral, Radiologist, Commander US Navy Reserves, Black Belt Combat Hapkido

Neil E. Farber, MD, PhD

THROW AWAY YOUR **VISION BOARD!**

The Truth about the Law of Attraction

Neil E. Farber, MD, PhD

Other books by Dr. Farber

The Blame Game: The Complete Guide to Blaming: How to Play and How to Quit. Bascom Hill Publishing, MN, 2010.

Making Lemonade: 101 Recipes to Convert Negatives into Positives. Dynamic Publishing Group, WI, 2013.

The No Blaming Zone: An allegorically true story about creating positive changes, harnessing energy, and achieving potential through the simple act of taking responsibility. Dynamic Publishing Group, WI, 2015.

The Financial Industry's Guide to The No Blaming Zone. Dynamic Publishing Group, WI, 2015.

- Check out Dr. Farber's **Blame Game** blog in the Happiness Section on PsychologyToday.com
- Like: www.facebook.com/TheActionBoard
- Check out **NeilFarber.com** to help establish and achieve your goals and your potential best you.
- Contact: Neil@NeilFarber.com

Throw Away Your Vision Board

THROW AWAY YOUR VISION BOARD!

The Truth about the Law of Attraction

Neil E. Farber, MD, PhD

CreateSpace Independent Publishing Group

Neil E. Farber, MD, PhD

Copyright ©2014 by Neil E. Farber, M.D., Ph.D.

CreateSpace Independent Publishing Platform, North Charleston, SC

All rights reserved. No part of this publication may be reproduced, stored in a retrieval system, or transmitted, in any form or by any means, electronic, mechanical, photocopying, recording or otherwise, without the prior written permission of the author.

Limit of Liability/Disclaimer of Warranty: While the publisher and author have used their best efforts in preparing this book, they make no representations or warranties with respect to the accuracy or completeness of the contents of this book and specifically disclaim any implied warranties of merchantability or fitness for a particular purpose. The advice and strategies contained herein may not be suitable for your situation. Consult with a professional where appropriate. Neither the publisher nor author shall be liable for any loss of profit or any other commercial damages, including but not limited to special, incidental, consequential, or other damages.

ISBN-13 978-1507847305
ISBN-10 1507847300
Library of Congress Control Number - 2015904186

Printed in the United States of America

Throw Away Your Vision Board

Neil E. Farber, MD, PhD

Contents

Dedication.. i
Acknowledgements... ii
Preface.. v

Vision Boards... 1

1. Vision Boards: History................................... 2
2. Vision Boards: The Good............................... 16
3. Vision Boards: The Bad and the Ugly............. 21
4. Metaphysical Pseudoscience........................... 25
5. No Purpose... 46
6. No Action... 51
7. No Plan.. 59
8. No Date.. 64
9. No Challenges.. 67
10. No Compassion... 70
11. No Support... 75
12. Mindless... 78
13. Blame Yourself... 89
14. Blame the Victim.. 94
15. We're Not Perfect... 99

16. The Placebo Effect...104

17. Anecdotal Evidence 108

18. Throw Away Your Vision Board............................. 117

Action Boards...................................**129**

19. Introduction to Action Boards.............................. 130

20. Principles: The Key to Achieve....…................... 135

21. Components 145

22. Conclusion..…........ 155

Index

About the Author

Dedication

I lovingly dedicate this book to my daughter Sarena Jordyn. Sarena is a kind and gentle soul. She treats strangers as friends and friends as family. When I looked up Intrinsic Happiness online, I found Sarena's picture. When I think of someone who sincerely experiences a love of life, I envision Sarena. Words that describe Sarena—Serene, Motivated, Driven, Creative, Loving, Altruistic, Joyful, and full of Inspired Action.

Acknowledgements

Kaelah, Shoshana, and Sarena—I love you all. You are beautiful examples of what it's like to take responsibility for your actions and travel a path of positivity.

Thank you to my parents, Linda and Michael (OBM) for teaching me that while words are important, action is more important. I wouldn't have been here to do this without your actions!

Deep appreciation to my positivity gurus: Tal Ben-Shahar, Ellen Langer, Martin Seligman, Jon Gordon, David Pollay, Mihaly Csikszentmihalyi, Barbara Fredrickson, Afton Hassett, Ed Diener, Sonja Lyubomirsky, Dan Gilbert, Jon Kabat-Zinn, and Deepak Chopra it is through your principles and teachings that I have developed the concept of The Action Board.

Spirituality fills my life with meaning and for that I am grateful to Rabbis Dovid, Menachem, and Moshe Rapoport, Mordechai Spalter, David Cooper, as well as The Dalai Lama and Thich Naht Hanh.

My martial arts mentors have taught me so much more about life and what it is to thrive rather than simply kick and punch. You are all Grandmasters of Inspired Action: John Pellegrini, Avi Nardia, Miki Erez, Moti Horenstein, Maurice Elmalem, Bill Wallace, Moni Isaac, Chaim Bachar, Chaim Peer, Dana Abbott, Park Sang Young, and Masters Mark Gridley, David Rivas, Paul Chay, and Donald Moore.

Drs. Joseph Kerschner, David Warltier, George Hoffman, and Steven Butz, my gurus in medicine who have supported my rather non-traditional pathway in medicine, you have encouraged me by bringing positive psychology into our practice and our hospitals. Thank you.

Much gratitude goes to Beth Morrison, Life Coach extraordinaire, your contributions to the development of the Action Board have been substantial.

To my good friend Rhonda. Your help, guidance, and assistance have been an invaluable source of energy and motivation. Your words and actions are extremely important and your edits meaningful.

Finally, I would like to thank my friends, clients, students, patients, and colleagues. I am so appreciative that you allow me into your lives. I have learned so much from all of you.

Neil E. Farber, MD, PhD

Preface

A vision board is a goal setting tool. It is used to help you clarify and maintain your focus on some life goal. It is really any sort of board displaying images that represent whatever you want to have, be, or do in your life. Vision boarding has achieved notoriety in the past few years and has become a major international industry.

Not all vision boards are created equal, however all vision boards are based on the law of attraction; the belief that the universe is designed such that like *always* attracts like, positive *always* attracts positive and negative *always* attracts negative.

The law of attraction was made popular by the book and movie *The Secret*. However, the concept is not new. Before *The Secret*, there was the book *Creative Visualization* that described the same phenomenon. Creation is a two-step process, create it in your mind and then the physical creation will naturally follow.

"From where did this law of attraction originate?"

The earliest descriptions that name this as a *law* were in the New Thought Movement of the early 1900s, although some will claim that the origins date back to antiquity. Like any law of the universe, the law of attraction is allegedly as strong as the law of gravity. It never fails. Whatever you put into the universe is what you will *always* receive from the universe. In other words, by virtue of being a natural or universal "law" it *always* works. Vision boards channel your positive energy and imagery to the universe to grant you all of your wishes via the law of attraction.

There are some vision board proponents who claim the power to achieve success lies within you and not the board itself. They view the board as an inspirational, motivational tool to assist in manifesting and focusing on your goal. While I applaud this effort, this is a misrepresentation of the law of attraction. So, if vision boards are the next best thing to sliced bread, why is this book called **Throw Away Your Vision Board**?

Millions of people have been involved in vision boarding in one form or another. According to Joyce Schwarz, bestselling author of *The Vision Board* book, there are three to four million people who have been involved in, or exposed to, her Vision Board Institute's teachings and writings. There are thousands of people who have anecdotally claimed success at achieving their goals by using vision boards. However, there are many more who have created 'unsuccessful' vision boards. Even Oprah Winfrey's vision board coach states she has created many boards, which were "complete failures."

Why are there so many disappointed and unfulfilled vision boarders? How is it possible for an expert to fail multiple times at achieving goals using a universal tool that always works? Perhaps the vision board is not the magic bullet it is purported to be.

Throughout my life, I have always had amazing personal success in achieving my goals. *Without* invoking the law of attraction, I have realized my goals of becoming a physician, obtaining a PhD degree and becoming a Psychology Professor, receiving multiple awards as a research scientist, attaining multiple black belts and certifications in various martial arts, winning many tournaments, teaching self-defense to the Israeli and US armies, publishing several books and over 150 articles, becoming a life coach and personal trainer, working at one of the best children's hospitals in the country, living in my dream house, having fabulous children, being financially well-off, loving my life, and so much more... Everything I've achieved has been without a vision board.

I wrote an article, which appeared in *Psychology Today*, titled, **"Throw Away Your Vision Board."** The article evoked many emotional responses, both positive and negative, from "You're absolutely correct, the whole concept is silly," to "How dare you question the law of attraction?" and "If you're doubting the law of attraction, then you really don't understand it."

After I finished writing my first book *The Blame Game*, I created a vision board. I sent the book to several well-known individuals for endorsements. I had heard about vision boards, and decided to make up a vision board about getting additional endorsements.

After creating my vision board, I wrote a letter to Rhonda Byrne, author of the book *The Secret*. I asked Ms. Byrne for an endorsement for my book. A letter arrived from one of her assistants stating Ms. Byrne did not do book endorsements. I responded with another letter stating it was not possible for her to refuse providing an endorsement because I had already visualized that it had happened. I had no doubts about it. I knew that she had done it. I received no response from their office.

For several months I waited, visualized, and believed Rhonda Byrne would send me an endorsement. I had done everything I was supposed to do—created a vision board, made it positive, specific, and focused, asked the universe, and behaved as though it had already happened. Then I realized this was not true because I took action. I sent her a letter asking for a recommendation—this meant I really knew that she had not yet done it. I also did not send the book out to get published because I wanted to wait for the endorsement. Thus, it was impossible to act as if it already happened and at the same time take any sort of action toward making it happen. I was trying to fool the universe. By the way, I'm still waiting for her endorsement.

The vision board sounded so easy to do: set a goal, make it specific, cut out representative pictures (ASK), imagine it has already happened (BELIEVE), and then wait for the Universe to give it to me (RECEIVE). But vision boards are like most things that sound too good to be true…

Am I qualified to be able to assess the law of attraction? Yes. I have successfully fulfilled many goals and teach classes and coach individuals on goal setting. I have studied every book I could find about the law of attraction from the late 1800s to the present day and I have even been certified as an *Advanced Practitioner of the Law of Attraction* by law of attraction expert Dr. Joe Vitale. Moreover, the law of attraction is said to be based on science—metaphysics, psychology and brain research. I am a trained research scientist and Professor who has studied metaphysics, mind-brain science, and psychology.

This book is not a mission to dispel beliefs in mysticism or spirituality. This does not preclude a belief in God and the power of the universe. The universe is energy and we are part of that energy. But just because the law of attraction is mystical, doesn't make it correct. A belief in the law of attraction has all of the validity of a belief in Santa, the Easter Bunny, or Magical Purple Flying Oorts.

Are you like so many people who have tried unsuccessfully to set up and follow a dream board or vision board? It sounded so good at the time. The advertisement told you how successful you would be and how easy it was to accomplish if you were truly focused and practiced visualizing, manifesting... But it didn't happen that way.

John Assaraf, a leading authority on vision boards and the law of attraction, claims the law of attraction does not work for 99.9% of the people who try to use it. He believes this is due to their beliefs, habits, and values not aligning; the conscious mind and subconscious mind not working in harmony. This is true. While you are trying to invoke the law of attraction and visualizing the perfect future, you can't also take the required action steps to fulfill your goals! It is not just that vision boards do not work better than other kinds of inspirational pictures. Furthermore, believing in the law of attraction may be detrimental to your health, waste time, inhibit compassion for others, decrease your motivation, and actually lessen your chance of success.

This book will first take you through a brief history of vision boards and the law of attraction. Next, we will look at the good, the bad, and the ugly side of vision boards—the negative consequences of putting your faith in the law of attraction. Finally, a new concept in goal-achieving tools, the Action Board, will be introduced.

The Action Board is an evidence-based system founded on ground-breaking research studies in social psychology, positive psychology, mind-brain science, and goal achievement. The fundamental bases of the Action Board are the eight Key to Achieve principles and ten components that re-train your brain, activate your focus center, and connect your conscious and subconscious minds to work in harmony. All of the successful 'experts' claiming to use the law of attraction actually use principles from the Action Board to achieve their personal goals. I first published this in *Psychology Today* in 2012. With about a quarter million hits, the Action Board is quickly gaining respect as the ultimate GOAL-ACHIEVEMENT BOARD.

The truth is that you don't have to **Throw Away Your Vision Board**. Don't waste the pictures and motivational sayings. Convert your vision board into an Action Board. You upgrade your car, cell phone, computer, iPad, and Microsoft Windows. Now is your chance to upgrade your goal board. This will be an empowering and energizing upgrade that will take you from spectator to participant in achieving your goals.

Visit www.TheKeytoAchieve.com
Facebook: www.facebook.com/TheActionBoard
Follow me on Twitter: @neilfarber

Section I

1

Vision Boards: History

The history of the vision board is not well documented. If you simply define a vision board as a collage of pictures that are somehow related to what you want, then you will find evidence of cave paintings from prehistoric times that probably fulfill these criteria. Using this definition, any picture or painting in history could be admitted to the vision board historic society.

In this regard, one may speculate, as Joyce Schwarz,[1] President of the Vision Board Institute, has done, that there is an association between vision boards and Egyptian hieroglyphics, South Pacific and Native American petroglyphs, coats of arms in the Middle Ages, Asian seals (inken), Renaissance paintings, and treasure maps from the Gold Rush era. Obviously, the multitude of disappointed followers of Gold Rush treasure maps is not the best advertisement for the success of vision boards.

Here are some significant writings and events in the history of the law of attraction. It is difficult to separate the history of the vision board from the history of the law of attraction.

The Bible:
Some law of attraction proponents will claim that God was the first to invoke the law of attraction during the creation of the world: "And God said, 'Let there be light', And there was light." (Genesis 1:3)

And so it was for the land and the sky, the beasts, and even man. The verbal command precludes the physical manifestation. There exist several other Old Testament (see the book of Psalms) and New Testament examples of this process. "Whatever things you desire when you pray, believe that you have received them and you shall have them." (Mark 11:24) The art of visualization is not restricted to Western Religions.

Roman:
Marcus Aurelius, the great Roman Emperor, said, "A man's life is what his thoughts make of it."

Buddhism:
Buddhism and Hinduism also utilize these creative forces. From Buddha's Dhammapada teaching: "All that is the result of thought; it is founded on thought, it is made of thought. If a man speaks or acts with a pure thought, happiness follows him, like a shadow that never leaves him." Buddhist Amityus describes specific visualization techniques to manifest ideal states of mind and Buddhist *metta* meditation utilizes visualization to project loving-kindness. This form of meditation is highly effective for improving empathy and decreasing stress and has been incorporated into mindfulness-based stress reduction courses.

New Thought:
While visualization has remained important in certain religious traditions throughout the ages, it wasn't until the New Thought Movement began in the 1800s that creative visualization took on a new life. The New Thought Movement, primarily a blend of

metaphysics and religious beliefs, promotes that Infinite Intelligence is everywhere, divine thought creates goodness, and all sickness originates in the mind.

Ralph Waldo Emerson:
While not often considered part of the New Thought Movement, Ralph Waldo Emerson may be credited with energizing the movement. In his 1837 speech for *The American Scholar*[2] he stated, "The sacredness which attaches to the act of creation, the act of thought…"

William James:
James, the godson of Emerson, was a psychologist, philosopher, and non-practicing physician. As a Professor at Harvard, his students included WEB Dubois, Gertrude Stein, and Theodore Roosevelt. Instrumental in bringing the New Thought Movement to the forefront, he wrote, "We need only in cold blood act as if the thing in question were real, and it will become infallibly real by growing into such a connection with our life that it will become real." He also wrote, "Man can alter his life by altering his thinking." It is interesting to note that in 1896 James addressed the philosophical clubs of Yale and Brown Universities and stated, "It is wrong always, everywhere, and for everyone, to believe anything upon insufficient evidence."

William James is also well known for his theory (1884) that emotion is the mind's perception of physiological conditions arising from some stimulus.[3] In other words, when we see a bear, we don't run because of fear. When we see a bear we run and, consequently, our minds' perception of the increased adrenaline, sweaty palms, higher blood pressure, and faster heartbeat produces the emotion of fear. We are afraid because we run! We are sad because we cry and we are scared because we tremble.

Emma Curtis Hopkins

Hopkins was a spiritual author, mystic, Christian Science practitioner, and the 'mother' of the New Thought Movement. She founded her own school of Metaphysical Science and in 1888 she authored *Class Lessons,*[4] *Drops of Gold* and *Scientific Christian Mental Practice.*

Prentice Mulford:

Prentice Mulford was unsuccessful at mining for gold, copper, or silver, unable to make a career in politics, and not well off financially, living as a hermit for 17 years. He became a humorist, comedian, and author who consolidated a central concept of the New Thought Movement in 1889, with his book, *Thoughts Are Things.*[5] This book served as a guide to the new belief system. He followed this up in 1907, with *Your Forces and How to Use Them*.

James Allen:

James Allen retired from the business world to become a prolific British writer known for his inspirational works, including his spiritual magazine. In 1902 he published his most famous work, *As a Man Thinketh*[6]. The title was based on the Biblical proverb, "As a man thinketh in his heart, so is he." While reportedly being an inspiration for *The Secret,* this book is more about the power of man to control his own destiny through positive thinking than hypothetical musings and metaphysical laws.

As a Man Thinketh is not about having the universe do anything for you—it's about personal responsibility. This book fits in more with a positive psychology viewpoint that your thoughts and beliefs determine your personal reality by shaping your character, habits, health and circumstances.

Thomas Troward:

Thomas Troward was a divisional judge in British-ruled India. Following his retirement, he began writing lectures on philosophy and comparative religion. He became President of the International New Thought Alliance and, in 1904, wrote about thought preceding physical form.[7] He stated, "the action of Mind plants that nucleus which, if allowed to grow undisturbed, will eventually attract to itself all of the conditions necessary for its manifestation in outward visible form." There is no credited scientific basis for Troward's conjectures and he had no known background in metaphysics. The movie, *The Secret,* later adapted into a bestselling book, credits its production to Troward's beliefs.

William Walker Atkinson:

William Walker Atkinson was an attorney, businessman, author, occultist and a primary architect of the law of attraction. After suffering a mental breakdown and financial disaster, he joined the New Thought Movement and began writing. With over 100 books in all, under several pseudonyms including Yogi Ramacharaka and

Swami Bhakta Vishita, Atkinson was also well known for his Psychic Club, School of Mental Science, and belief in the occult.

In 1900, as an associate editor of *Suggestion* magazine, he wrote, *Thought-Force in Business and Everyday Life*.[8] Following this, in 1906, he authored the book *Thought Vibration or the Law of Attraction in the Thought World*[9] in which he stated, "The Universe is governed by Law – one great Law...Like attracts like."

That same year he also wrote the book, *Dynamic Thought, or the Law of Vibrant Energy*.[10] In this book he conjectures some of the basic tenets of the law of attraction. "...the Basis for All Energy, Force, and Motion." Atkinson was very clever in using circular arguments to state a hypothesis, using this hypothesis to "prove" further supporting statements, and eventually using those "proofs" to confirm the original hypothesis. Atkinson introduced us to his views of thought particles flying off the brain of the thinker and how thinking leads to a "burning up" of brain matter, which forms a "high vibratory power." He claimed that these are truths known by physiologists. In fact, these 'truths' are merely fantasies and in no way represent scientific knowledge.

Bruce MacLelland:

The Nautilus, a journal of New Thought, published Bruce MacLelland's book, *Prosperity Through Thought Force*[11] *(1907)*. In this book he professes, "That the mind attracts success in all things as it is freed from jealousy, envy, distrust, ill will, anger, haste and fear."

MacLelland was a bookkeeper turned author who claimed "...that through introspection, mental suggestions, the Law of

Vibration and the power of imagination, anyone can make of himself whatever he chooses." He continued, "Thoughts are vital, living, actual things, as real as oxygen or hydrogen." MacLelland asserts, "We know that **all** advice, logical or illogical, is a useless waste of energy, and that the knowledge of these things will not assist you in the least..." He also felt that as long as you invoke the law of attraction, change your attitude, practice optimism, seek peace and read your Bible, you will achieve what you want.

MacLelland states the proof for the law of attraction was "well understood by Joseph, Moses and the Christ of Jewish history." MacLelland writes he achieved success through repeating self-suggestions: "I **fear** nothing." "I shall never **worry** over anything." "Nothing will **burden** me." "I cannot help being **worried** over the future." "I must forget my **troubles**." "Well, it cannot **harm** me to try." "No one will laugh at me if I **fail**." "I am **tired** of **this condition** and shall better it." Most present-day proponents of the law of attraction would claim that the universe would hear all of these negative terms and bring him more negativity.

It is also curious that he wrote, "I have moments of depression, of loss of confidence in self, lack of faith in God, as well as the occasional inability to sustain a happy buoyancy and contentment of mind." Despite this, he claims that he was able to achieve all of his monetary needs and a happy home. Apparently, having all of his thoughts, feelings, emotions, habits, and behavior aligned in a positive way was not important for his success through the law of attraction. This appears to be a double standard. Think negative thoughts and use negative words, yet still achieve all of his goals by invoking the law of attraction? Why can't the rest of us do this?

As a side note, MacLelland also felt this "law" did not just apply to humans. "Spotted buildings and fences cause an increase in the number of spotted cattle on the farm." Oh, of course!

Wallace Wattles:

The Science of Getting Rich[12] (1910), by Wallace Wattles, is one of the classic books of the New Thought Movement. It was this book that supposedly influenced Rhonda Byrne to create the film *The Secret*. Wattles proposed when you believe in the object of your desire and focus on it, you will be led to that object or goal being realized. Similarly, negative thinking will manifest negative results. Wattles expects the reader to "take the fundamental statements upon faith, just as he would take statements concerning a law of electrical action if they were promulgated by a Marconi or an Edison…" Wattles further states,

- *"…it is not possible to live a really complete or successful life unless one is rich. No man can rise to his greatest possible height in talent or soul development unless he has plenty of money."*
- *"We live in a thought world, which is part of a thought universe. The thought of a moving universe extended throughout Formless Substance, and the Thinking Stuff moving according to that thought, took the form of systems of planets, and maintains that form."*
- *"…the thought of an oak tree does not cause the instant formation of a full-grown tree, but it does start in motion the forces which will produce the tree…"*

Wattles was an unsuccessful candidate for political office with the Socialist Party of America and was banished from the Methodist

Church for heresy. Of note, Wattles' daughter wrote that he was extremely frail in the last three years before his death (in 1911 at age *51*). It remains unclear as to why Wattles did not make use of the law of attraction to prevent his illness from occurring and to optimize his health.

Napoleon Hill:

One of the most influential sources for the law of attraction was Napoleon Hill. In 1908, Hill, a reporter, was given the job of interviewing Andrew Carnegie—one of the most successful men in the world. Carnegie, in turn, challenged Hill to interview other highly successful men and women. In the *Law of Success in Sixteen Lessons*[13] *(1928),* Hill proposed that the law of attraction was operated by use of radio waves transmitted by the brain. He also focused on several valuable lessons including taking initiative, developing self-confidence, enthusiasm, self-control, focusing your attention, and profiting by failure—yours and that of others.

Hill believed the fluid portion of all that vibrates was universal in nature. He erroneously conjectured the only difference between sound, light, heat, and thought was the rate of fluid vibration. Hill theorized the mind was made of ether and our brains become magnetized with dominating thoughts. These magnets attract us to like-minded people, things, and situations in the universe. *This is the foundational scientific basis for the law of attraction;* unfounded hypotheses based on what 'seems to be possible'.

Hill emphasized *all diseases* begin when the brain is depleted or in a devitalized state. He mentions sexual contact is a great means of revitalizing an exhausted brain and that is why all great leaders are highly sexed.

Hill published *Think and Grow Rich*[14] (1937), one of the bestselling books in history, in which he expands his discussion about the energy that thoughts have and their ability to attract other thoughts. One of his best-known sayings is, "Whatever your mind can conceive and believe it can achieve." Hill's predominant message was living with a PMA—a positive mental attitude.[15]

Hill's personal life consisted of a great deal of ups and downs, both financially and personally. It is in *Think and Grow Rich* that a *secret* is introduced. Hill tells the story of a money-making secret given to him by Carnegie. Although he doesn't call it by name, Hill states he mentioned the secret no fewer than 100 times throughout the book; at least once in every chapter. In performing a complete analysis of this book, the word "attraction" is used only 3 times. The word "attract" is used 21 times. It doesn't appear likely that law of attraction was the *secret* to Hill's success. In contrast, the words "act" or "action" are used exactly 100 times—more on this later.

Earl Nightingale:

As a salesman and broadcaster, Nightingale was influenced by Napoleon Hill. In 1959, he recorded *The Strangest Secret*.[16] Nightingale looked at the behaviors and attitudes of the five percent of people who succeeded at achieving their goals and concluded, "We become what we think about." Nightingale suggested you "Act as though it were impossible to fail."

W. Clement Stone:

Co-author of *Success Through a Positive Mental Attitude* with Napoleon Hill, Stone was the prototypical story of rags to riches. He transformed from impoverished to multimillionaire, making his money in the insurance industry. Rather than focus on mysticism, Stone dedicated his life to encouraging others to take control and do what they can. In 1962, Stone wrote *The Success System That Never Fails*. Superficially, this would seem to be like many of the other law of attraction books that guarantee success. However, this book actually concentrates on practical tips and strategies that you should employ to achieve success. For example, Stone suggests, "Inspiration to action is the most important ingredient to success in any human activity. And inspiration to action can be developed at will."[17]

Shakti Gawain:

Gawain was a teacher who studied psychology and philosophy in her quest for personal development. In her book *Creative Visualization*[18] (1978), she introduced the concept of treasure maps (vision boards). She explained how to use mental imagery and positive affirmations to bring about desired changes in your life. The book focuses on the power of imagination and channeling your energy; concentrating more on your power to visualize than on the power of the universe.

Bob Proctor:

Proctor, a firefighter in Toronto, was inspired by Hill's *Think and Grow Rich*. He became a successful businessman and moved to Chicago where he worked with Earl Nightingale. In 1984 Proctor wrote *You are Born Rich*.[19] In this book, he expanded on the role of the law of vibration and the law of attraction. He describes the brain as "simply a vibratory instrument." Proctor asserts that everything in the universe is connected to everything else through the law of vibration. He suggests one must only choose to vibrate positively. Interestingly, despite these recommendations, Proctor also suggests that when establishing a new goal, you should set up a balance sheet with the benefits on one side and the "very worst thing that could happen to you" on the other. This doesn't sound like a very 'positive-only' focus.

Rhonda Byrne:

Byrne was a television producer who received a copy of Wattle's *The Science of Getting Rich*. In both movie and book form (2006) she wrote about the law of attraction as *The Secret*.[20] This was the first and biggest mass media exposure for the law of attraction and instigated a new vision board industry. It specified the steps of Ask, Believe and then Receive. Following this, Oprah Winfrey devoted two episodes of her talk show to *The Secret*, discussing the law of attraction, and she even got a vision board coach.

Hicks:

In 2008, Esther and Jerry Hicks published *Money and the Law of Attraction: Learning to Attract Health, Wealth & Happiness*.[21] Jerry, a former circus performer, musician and comedian, began using Hill's book of success to help his Amway business distribution. He married Esther, who, after reading the channeling works of Jane Roberts, also reported receiving messages from beyond. Esther claimed to channel a "group of entities," "infinite intelligence" and a "group consciousness from the non-physical dimension" named Abraham. Their book helped transform the law of attraction from thought patterns travelling through the ether to a thinking and feeling universe, which "adores" people and knows their intentions.

Esther Hicks originally had a significant role in the movie *The Secret*, but this was eliminated when there were significant contract disputes with Rhonda Byrne. Obviously, not everyone received all that they desired from the universe during this disagreement. Like authors before her, she believes that you create with every thought.

The Hickses also believe 1) People cannot die; their lives are everlasting, 2) All illnesses, diseases, and accidents are caused by ill/dysfunctional thoughts, 3) Modern medicine is not needed and is, in fact, counterproductive, 4) "Any disease could be healed in a matter of days" by thoughts. Despite these teachings, when Jerry Hicks developed cancer (reported by Hicks to be a spider bite), he secretly underwent what he later termed "heavy chemotherapy" and died in 2011.

Other Authors:

A few other notable books should be mentioned. John Assaraf's *The Vision Board Book*[22] and Joyce Schwarz's, *The Vision Board*.[1] Both of these books described several facets of vision boards that include the law of attraction, as well as expressing gratitude and taking action. Assaraf's book also described the importance of choosing goals not just based on superficial wants, but on your deep-seated values to help set up more profound intentions.

Many authors have written hundreds of similar books on the law of attraction such as:

- Jack Canfield: *Key to Living the Law of Attraction.*[23] Interestingly, even though it says focus on the positive, he still recommends making up a chart with things you want and things you don't want. This is in contrast to what he suggests in *The Secret*. He also mentions that thoughts are "measurable units of energy," although he offers no evidence for this.
- Meera Lester: *365 Ways to Live the Law of Attraction.*[24] One-a-day suggestions.
- Dr. Robert Worstell: *Secrets to the Law of Attraction.*[25] You need to take action. Note; this is contrary to the law of attraction.
- Joe Vitale: *The Key: The Missing Secret for Attracting Anything You Want*[26] and *The Attractor Factor.*[27] Focuses on why relying on such a great law is often not enough.

The *secret* is that all of these books repeat and expand on hypothetical conjectures in metaphysics (as you'll see in Chapters 3 through 18). While many of the consequences of those conjectures are quite helpful, such as a focus on positivity, the belief in the law of attraction is unnecessary, and, in fact, counterproductive.

2

Vision Boards: The Good

Vision boards, also known as dream boards, life boards, life collages, vision collages, treasure maps, vision maps, and wish boards, are terms given to a collection of pictures, photos, collages, and motivational slogans placed onto a flat surface.

Millions of people around the world use vision boards in an effort to establish and attain their goals. While they were made popular by the movie and book *The Secret*,[1] the process of visualizing your highest priorities and dreams has been around for a long time (see previous chapter on history). Since *The Secret* there have been dozens, if not hundreds, of books, online sites, and businesses that have adapted, modified, and capitalized on these concepts. However, the one common theme regarding vision boards is that they all utilize the theory of the law of attraction; what you put into the universe, you will get back.

As stated in the preface to this book, I do realize and appreciate that there are many different shades and varieties of vision boards. There are some vision boards that incorporate newer, research-based findings regarding goal setting. Some vision boards are remarkably similar to the Action Board that I have created (more about this in Section 2) in that they have comparable beliefs in certain key principles. However, despite many commonalities, there is one critical issue that limits the usefulness of all vision boards. This is the belief and reliance on the law of attraction. Chapters 3 and 4 will focus on why this is such a critical issue.

There are some redeeming concepts and applications of vision boards that will help you establish goals and visualize your dreams. Here are what I consider to be the 'good' things about vision boards:

1. *It's easy*: As John Assaraf, vision board expert and contributor to *The Secret*, has written in *The Complete Vision Board Kit*,[2] "Creating your own vision board is easy…" However, as he correctly points out, just discussing the vision board doesn't tell the whole story about goal achievement. The vision board is one goal setting tool, the essential ingredients are the principles that go into creating your board.

2. *It's fun*: Creating a vision board is great stress relief, allowing you to get in touch with your creative side. Rummage through magazines looking for pictures, photos, or motivational sayings that have deep personal meaning. It will seem like you are back in grade school doing an art project or collage, bringing out your inner child.

3. *Multiple Goals*: While many books about the law of attraction deal predominantly with how to set goals for wealth, financial success, and material goods, the vision board may also be used for other types of goals, such as finding life partners, improving relationships, conflict management, health-related issues, and athletic challenges.

4. *Personalized*: There is no "correct" way to build a vision board. Vision boards are highly personalized, delving into your creative soul to "choose" how your board will appear.

5. ***Bring clarity***: Vision boards create clarity and help delineate what it is that you want to be, do, or get. Many of us spend a lot of time bouncing from goal to goal and from activity to activity, without any sort of direction. Constructing a vision board takes little effort and certainly brings a more precise definition to your goal.

6. ***Purpose***: Some, but not all vision boards invoke a sense of purpose. Why do you want to achieve this goal? In truth, most vision boards I have encountered do not spend time on this component of goal setting. Instead, goals are often chosen by meaningful images that come to you while you are meditating or spiritually in touch with your inner soul. John Assaraf does a great job, encouraging people to choose their goals based on their values, not just their wants. As *The Complete Idiot's Guide to Vision Boards*[3] suggests, the images and phrases that make the board should represent your highest priorities.

7. ***Positive Focus***: Based on the law of attraction, a negative person putting out negative energy will receive negativity from the universe. If you exude positive energy and think only positive thoughts, the universe will provide positive rewards. Our beliefs, thoughts, emotions, and actions draw to us situations, people, and things with a similar vibrational frequency. Depending on the type of vision board that you are making, this can vary from simply having a positive mental attitude and pretending that things are positive (as proposed in *The Secret* and by several law of attraction authors) to adjusting your habits, behaviors, and beliefs to align with your positive attitude. There is another way this exact same effect can be derived without invoking the law of attraction. More on this later.

8. *Gratitude*: In the vision board process, you are not alone in your quest to achieve your dreams. The universe is your partner in this journey. The law of vibration dictates that you are responsible for what you think and how your brain cells, and consequently your thoughts, vibrate. However, the universe is a caring and adoring associate. It will give to you what you show it you really want. To complete the act of receiving, you should focus on gratitude. Be thankful to the universe for allowing you to accomplish your goals (even if you haven't actually done that yet) and for what you already possess. This will show the universe you are appreciative and positive and the universe will give you more of the same, more things for which to be grateful. There are many health and wellness benefits associated with gratitude including living longer, being happier, and even an enhanced immune system!

9. *Attention and Focus*: One of the main purposes of vision boards is to help you delineate your desires and convert them into some tangible form. You develop an energetic bond with what you believe you really want out of life and then visualize yourself in this place. Creating a board, as I said, is easy and fun. To successfully bring yourself to a future place where you have achieved your goal and you now live in that place as if it were the present, is not so easy. It requires a great deal of attention and focus to stay in that role. Remember, it is only in that role, living and acting as if you've already achieved your goal, that you are showing the universe that you have no doubts. Please carefully read the book *The Secret* and original texts of the law of attraction to verify these statements.

Some vision board and law of attraction proponents claim that you don't need to stay in this role for very long. Practice it about one half hour per day and the rest of the day work on other goal achieving behaviors. However, if you really believe in the law of attraction: 1) there is no need to do anything else to achieve your goal 2) any action or planning toward your goal demonstrates doubt—negativity 3) any planning or action toward your goal shows that you admit to the universe that you have not achieved it yet—dishonesty is negative.

10. *Mental Imagery*: As above, in order to sufficiently show the universe you have faith in its ability to provide and help you create through your thoughts, you should think about your goals as if they've already occurred. In other words, act and live as if you've accomplished exactly what you want to become, what you wish to obtain, or what you'd like to achieve. There is a great deal of scientific research that has demonstrated the power and benefits of mental imagery. However, there is much more to this story than I am describing in this section. Studies show that not all ways of visualizing are equally effective. I am leaving the best for later when I describe these studies in more detail to allow you to visualize in the most effective way possible. The secret to effective visualization will be disclosed in Chapters 12 and 20.

3

Vision Boards: The Bad and The Ugly

If concepts such as visualization, positivity, gratitude, and bringing clarity to your purpose are desirable features of vision boards, what is so bad about them? This next section will prove to you that when you dive deeper into the principles, the typical vision board may not only be inadequate, it actually may be counterproductive for your goal achieving needs.

I realize that just reading these words is akin to blasphemy for some. I have heard these comments before:
- "How dare you criticize the law of attraction!"
- "The only people who criticize vision boards are those who do not fully understand them."
- "You are too entrenched in science to just let go and have faith in the universe."
- "You obviously don't have any understanding of the law of attraction."

Here is my response to these comments:

1) I have read almost every book written about the law of attraction, especially foundational books that were written in the late 1800s and early 1900s. In contrast to many so-called experts, I have actually gone back to the sources and original texts that invented this law and analyzed the details of what they have proposed. I would venture to say I have thoroughly read as many books on the law of attraction as any other "expert" in the world.

2) I have extensively studied the law of attraction with one of the foremost experts in the field, Dr. Joe Vitale. Dr. Vitale is prominently featured as a contributor in the book and movie, *The Secret*.[1] He has written several law of attraction books himself. Following these courses of study, Dr. Vitale certified me as an "Advanced Practitioner of The Law of Attraction".

3) It is true that I am a scientist and physician and tend to look at information with a discerning eye: a skeptic, if you will. This is to say I don't want to waste my time and energy doing tasks and rituals that have no benefit. I look for proof. So it was vitally important to me to complete a full analysis of the law of attraction in all aspects and from a variety of perspectives. Recognize that a skeptic is different from a cynic. As one of the world's leading skeptics, Michael Shermer[2] has argued that skeptics are not cynical. They are open-minded, looking for evidence to prove or disprove a theory.

4) While I do have a PhD in research, I also believe in alternative medicine (I was the chairman of an alternative medicine committee at my hospital), meditation, and the power of spirituality for both psychological as well as physical healing. I am a firm believer in the benefits and power of mindfulness and have completed a fabulous mindfulness-based stress reduction (MBSR) course and I've been certified in mindfulness-based cognitive-behavioral therapy. I teach meditation and mindfulness classes and have used these techniques for my own personal healing of physical traumas as well as previously debilitating arthritis.

5) I challenge those of you who are insulted by my investigation into the law of attraction to do what you accuse me of not doing. Be open-minded. When I began looking into the law of attraction, I was hoping this would be something effective because it would be fun and simple to do. Alas, I am sorry I found out that the law of attraction does not exist. Please read the chapters in the next section with an open heart and an open mind.

6) Keep in mind I am not being critical of being positive. I am not being critical of visualization. There are many amazing benefits to the process of visualization; but, again, not all visualization is created equal. There are several issues with traditional vision boards that make them less effective than what could be possible, given the amazing power of visualization (see Chapters 12 and 20).

7) The law of attraction is a scientific theory. All of its proponents have treated it as such, making multiple specific (and often outlandish) chemical, anatomical, physiological, and medical claims. As a scientific theory, the law of attraction should stand up to scientific scrutiny. As someone who has been trained as a neuroscientist, physician, and pharmacologist, I will show there is no physical evidence supporting the foundational basis for the law of attraction. Being a supposition of pseudoscientific conjectures does not necessarily make this system "bad". However, the law of attraction has become a scheme to sell to those less knowledgeable in energetic and scientific systems.

Many people have been critical of the book *The Secret*[1] and critical of Esther Hicks for relying on the universe and the law of attraction to do all of the work. The truth is that their interpretations of the law of attraction are accurate. This is also true of all of the contributors to *The Secret*, many of whom have gone on to become experts in this law with their own re-interpretations. Most of these interpretations involve planning and taking action. This is inconsistent with the original descriptions of the law of attraction.

There is a huge discrepancy between what works for these successful individuals and what they report. To incorporate techniques that they know to be valuable in goal-achievement, they modify the universal law of attraction in ways that lessen its role and give each of us more responsibility in reaching our goals and realizing our dreams. With so many people unsuccessfully trying to use vision boards, reported to be so easy, the "experts" have continually given us more hints and secrets and secrets to the secrets, rather than admit that this charade is over.

We no longer need to invoke any law of attraction. It isn't necessary and actually inhibits our growth. We can replace it with something better. The following chapters (4 through 17) will look in detail at why we should put the law of attraction into its final resting place. It did a great job in helping people incorporate a positive mental attitude into their daily lives and in promoting the art of creative visualization. Now, let it go…

The next chapter will specifically address some of the background theories of the law of attraction including, "Thought-stuff", "formless stuff", "thought-particles", "thought-waves", "master minds", etc. If it seems weird now, you don't know the half of it.

4

Metaphysical Pseudoscience

The law of attraction is a scientific theory based on disproven science, unfounded scientific theory, beliefs, and assumptions. Followers of and believers in the law of attraction view this law as immutable and accurate, without hearing any facts. Saying that something is true does not make it so. The authors of the law of attraction use unsupported ideas to support more unusual claims. They then use conclusions based on these assumptions to state that the initial hypothesis must be true.

If the law of attraction is confusing to you, you are not alone. A full understanding is not possible, as the underlying premise of the law of attraction does not make sense. This is about both poor science and faulty reasoning. The law of attraction is based upon inaccurate suppositions that were loosely connected, taken as fact, and then used to form an unsubstantiated conclusion. As a warning, some of the science will be unclear. My main purpose in presenting this is for you to appreciate the foundational basis for the law. Pay more attention to the reasoning; the use of **"suppose"** and **"if"** leading to definitive inferences. Vision board experts pride themselves on declaring that the law of attraction is science, not mysticism. So let's examine some of the science.

We'll start with some statements from one of the founders of the law of attraction, William Atkinson.[1] Some great examples of unfounded scientific hypotheses.

- "**Suppose** we call it 'The Law of Attraction,' of which Gravitation, Cohesion, Adhesion, Chemical Affinity, or Chemism are but different aspects."

Comment: A supposition without any basis—no evidence that these phenomena share any common law – or law of attraction.

- "…**if** Molecular Cohesion, and the vibrations accompanying it, manifest in forms of "Molecular Motion,"–and **if** Atomic "Chemical Affinity, or Chemism," manifest in "Atomic Motion"–and **if** even the Corpuscles in their movements obey this same "Law of Attraction" in some form – and **if** all Force and Energy is but a "Mode of Motion" – then, **if** all this be true, are we not justified in claiming this "Law of Attraction" is the Basis for All Energy, Force, and Motion?"

Comment: If we accept his hypothesis of atomic motion from chemism, we should also accept the law of attraction as the basis for ALL energy, force, and motion. In other words, here's hypothesis "A". Now, what if "A" influenced "D"? If "D" influenced "F" and if "F" influenced "T" and if "T" affected "W" then wouldn't you agree that "A" influences all of the other letters?

- "…from the above, it follows that: All Manifestations of Force and Energy in Inorganic Substance (viz., both Radiant Energy in its forms of Light, Heat, Magnetism, Electricity, etc.) and also Attractive Energy in its forms Gravitation, Cohesion, Adhesion, Chemical Affinity or Atomic Attraction and Corpuscular Attraction arise from the operation of the Law of Attraction."

Comment: Since we've assumed that the law of attraction exists and that it controls all forces and energy, it stands to reason that you would now believe it also controls every form of energy including light, heat, electricity, etc.

- "The mind of a thinker is constantly emitting or throwing off these particles of "Thought-stuff"; the distance and rate of speed, to and by which they travel, being determined by the "force" used in their production, there being a great difference between the thought of a vigorous thinker and that emanating from a weak, listless mind...Some remain around the place where they were emitted, while others float off like clouds, and obey the Law of Attraction which draws them to persons thinking along similar lines."

Comment: Suppose thinking causes thought-stuff to leave your brain. Suppose that it obeys the law of attraction.

- "These particles of "Thought-stuff" fly off from the brain of the thinker, in all directions, and affect other persons who may come into contact with them."

Comment: More baseless specifics about thought-stuff. There is no evidence for thought particles leaving the brain and affecting others.

- "Besides the operation of these particles of Thought-stuff emitted during the production of Thought, there are many other phases of Thought Influence, or Thought in Action. The principle phase of this phenomenon arises from the working of the Law of Attraction between the respective minds of different people."

Comment: **If** we believe there is thought-stuff and if we suppose there is the law of attraction, then you should believe that this same phenomenon works between individuals.

- "In the first place, it is a fact well known and accepted by investigators that the generation of Thought and the manifestation of Mental States occasions a 'burning up' of brain matter, and the consequent production of a form of energy of high vibratory power. Physiologists recognize this fact, and the textbooks make reference to it".[2]

Comment: There is no evidence that thinking causes "burning up" of brain matter and the creation of high vibratory energy.

Let's look at some specific scientific suppositions; what law of attraction proponents believe compared to what we know based on scientific evidence. "What we know" is derived from several sources.[3-9]

1. Electron charges

<u>What they believe</u>: Electrons have positive and negative charges.

<u>What we know</u>: Electrons are negatively charged and protons positively charged.

2. All forces are the same

<u>What they believe</u>: Gravity is an example of the law of attraction. All similar material things from subatomic particles to planets are drawn together.

<u>What we know</u>: Gravity is *not* an example of like attracts like. Non-charged objects are brought together by gravity. Universal laws are, in fact, *less* likely to attract objects of similar charges; *not* like attracts like. There may exist a massless graviton particle that pulls objects together or, according to Einstein, gravity is the distortion of space that alters the course of objects from traveling in a straight line. Gravity is very important at the macroscopic level, yet has little

influence at the subatomic level, where electromagnetism is critical. In contrast to the law of attraction, these two forces are not the same.

3.   Air and Ether

ABrown_What they believe_: The space between the sun, moon, stars and other planets of the universe is filled with ether. This ether keeps all matter in motion. About 50 miles from Earth is air. Thought can only be transmitted in ether; air conducts only sound vibrations, not light or higher vibrations like thought.

What we know: There are so many erroneous statements here that it is tough to know what to address first. There is no significant amount of ether in the atmosphere. Air is all around us; it does not start 50 miles up. Sound does transmit through air. It is highly unlikely that thought can be transmitted through ether. If anyone wants to be submerged into a vat of ether and try it out, please let me know—as an anesthesiologist, I can try to arrange this for you.

4.   Oxygen and altitude

What they believe: The higher you go, the more oxygen is in the air, which is why there are no plants at very high altitudes and why tubercular patients should be sent to high altitudes.

What we know: Oxygen levels decrease, not increase, as you increase altitude. High altitudes are hypoxic (low oxygen) environments—not healthy for any patient.

5.   Your brain on ether

What they believe: Our brains are composed of ether and our minds are transmitters and receivers.

What we know: Your brain is not composed of ether. It is a tight network of nerve cells, nerve fibers, and vascular and connective tissue. Your brain does generate an electrical field but thought waves are not brain waves. There is no evidence that our brain transmits to anything that is able to receive such a small signal with a high signal to noise ratio.

6. *Fluid in matter*

<u>What they believe</u>: In every particle of matter there is an invisible "fluid" that causes atoms to circle around one another at an inconceivable rate of speed. This fluid is a form of energy that is the same as electricity.

<u>What we know</u>: Quantum mechanics (the science of subatomic particles) has identified a wave-particle dualistic nature where subatomic particles exhibit both particle and wave traits. The story of subatomic energy is very complex. In part, it involves particles that transmit forces such as bosons. Also, electrons in atoms and molecules can change energy levels, emitting electromagnetic radiation (photons). Energy is produced in discrete packages (quanta) not continuously as predicted by the law of attraction.

7. *Vibration rates of fluid*

<u>What they believe</u>: One rate of fluid energy vibration causes sound. Vibrating faster, it becomes heat then light (above 3,000,000 vibrations/sec). Faster yet and it results in thought. Sound, light, heat, and thought are different versions of the same thing.

<u>What we know</u>: Not even close! Sound, light, heat, and thought are not the same thing. First, light and sound are not the same form of energy or on a continuum. Sound needs a medium in which to travel, light does not. Light is an electromagnetic wave of photons and may travel in a vacuum. Thicker media speed up sound and slow down

light. There is no sound in a vacuum because there's nothing to oscillate. In addition, there is a huge difference in the wave velocity, not just frequency. Sound waves are longitudinal and travel through air at about 1,100 *feet*/sec. On the other hand, light, composed of transverse waves, travels through air at about 186,000 *miles*/sec. In terms of heat, this is dynamic energy derived primarily from infrared electromagnetic waves, although it can also be during some visible light (overlap of energy frequencies). Heat involves physical matter moving around in an excited state. Thought is not known to be related to any of these energies.

8. Limits of our senses
<u>What they believe</u>: The human ear can only detect sound produced from 32,000 - 38,000 vibrations/sec.
<u>What we know</u>: Way off! The human ear can detect sound from about 20 Hz (vibrations/sec) to 20,000 Hz (i.e. the pressure in your ear oscillates back and forth 20 to 20,000 times/sec). Each frequency gives a different pitch (slower vibrations = lower notes). Dogs detect from 45–45,000 Hz, cats from 45–85,000, bats as high as 120,000 Hz and dolphins as high as 200,000 Hz.

9. Light and Sound
<u>What they believe</u>: Light is the same type of energy as sound, just with faster vibrations at 1.5 million – 3 million Hz.
<u>What we know</u>: As above, light and sound are completely different forms of energy. It is not just a matter of frequencies. They are qualitatively different. This is very important in terms of the law of attraction, since law of attraction proponents believe that thought is in the same continuum. Electromagnetic wave frequencies are more

than double (visible light $4 \times 10^{14} - 8 \times 10^{14}$ Hz) those predicted by law of attraction proponents.

10. Thought frequencies

What they believe: Thought frequencies could be between 40,000 Hz and 4×10^{14} Hz or above 7×10^{14} Hz since we don't know what's in those ranges. They are incredibly fast.

What we know: Not true. Between 40 kHz (4×10^4 Hz and 400 GHz (4×10^{11} Hz) is infrared electromagnetic radiation—NOT THOUGHT. Above 700 GHz are many other forms of electromagnetic radiation that were unknown at the time of the founding of the law of attraction. We now know of near ultraviolet, extreme ultraviolet, X rays, and gamma rays with vibrations up to about 300 EHz (300 x 10^{18} Hz). Therefore, there are no thought energies found up to this amazing level of vibrations.

Thoughts may be determined, not by content or information within an electrical impulse, but in the structure and pathways of the nerve fibers. As computers provide information as impulses, the information signal in the brain may be the same irrespective of the content. Brain waves are slow, operating in the 1 – 100 Hz frequency range. This happens to overlap with extremely low frequency radio waves (3 – 30 Hz).

Here is a very brief discussion about specific brain waves:

Delta waves (<4Hz): are very slow. They are associated with dreamless sleep and some attentional tasks.

Theta waves (4-8 Hz): occur during encoding, memory retrieving and light sleep.

Alpha waves (8-13 Hz): happen when you're relaxed or during focused attention.

Beta waves: (13-30 Hz): are seen during stimulation and when you're wide-awake.

Gamma waves (30 – 100 Hz): are associated with learning and idea formation.

Transmitting this very low power output information from the brain (microvolts at best) would be difficult because very little information would be transmitted at a time.

11. **Thought energy**

What they believe: Thought is a form of energy on a continuum with sound, light, and heat. It is fluid and magnetized.

What we know: There is no evidence for the concept of thought energy on a continuum with any other form of energy. There is no evidence that a magnetized or even electromagnetic thought-specific energy exists at all.

12. **Thought-stuff, thought particles**

What they believe: Thought particles (thought-stuff) are produced in the brain.

What we know: Thought particles do not exist.

13. **Thoughts are tangible things**

What they believe: Every thought has a unique neuropeptide (protein-based amino acid) associated with it. Your hypothalamus (in your brain) produces unique neuropeptides, associated with specific emotions, every time you have a thought.

What we know: It may be reasonable to postulate specific neuropeptides that are *emotion*-specific, although this has not been conclusively demonstrated. There is *NO* evidence that there are *thought-specific* neuropeptide sequences.

14.   Thought-stuff leaves the brain when you think
<u>What they believe</u>**:** Thinking causes "Thought-stuff," an "ethereal substance" to be emitted from your brain.
<u>What we know</u>: There are no particles of thought-stuff emitted while you are thinking. There are low energy electrical waves, as seen by electroencephalography (EEG), which may be detected at the scalp surface.

15.   Your thought-stuff affects other people
<u>What they believe</u>**:** Thought-stuff leaves your brain, travels around the world, and lasts forever. It interacts with other people and influences their thoughts and beliefs.
<u>What we know</u>: There is *no* evidence for any thought particles leaving the body or traveling any distance and controlling others' thoughts. Some electrical activity "leaks" out of our brains and can be detected by cortical or scalp EEG electrodes. It's hard to hypothesize that those impulses transmit any form of information. These are "brain" waves, not thought waves.

The human brain has a very, very low power output. Brain EEG produces very weak fields outside of the cranium and the human brain is very insensitive to all kinds of electromagnetic fields, including fields of this wavelength. Reading an EEG is more like reading an electric meter on your house than it is like a manual of your specific thoughts, since the signal-to-noise ratio is so high.

16. Perpetual transmission

<u>What they believe</u>: The law of perpetual transmission and transmutation of energy is the "first law of the universe." This is how a person of low energy gets energy from you and becomes "recharged" due to your thought vibrations. Everything you hear, see, taste, think, and even *feel* comes from energy that transmutes and transmits. The non-physical is always moving into physical form.

<u>What we know</u>: There is no evidence for this law of perpetual transmission. Yes, there is conservation of energy; there is constant motion and change in the universe. Extending this to our ability to recharge someone's thoughts is unfounded.

17. Vibrating brain cells

<u>What they believe</u>: Thoughts cause brain cells to vibrate and send off electromagnetic waves. Stronger thoughts mean faster vibrations and more potent electric waves.

<u>What we know</u>: I have actually measured and recorded activity from brain cells. There is no known correlation between thought intensity and brain cell vibration. Focusing thoughts increases regional cerebral blood flow due to increases in neuronal activity and neurochemical transmissions. This is unrelated to vibrating brain cells or more potent electric waves.

18. Anger Cells

<u>What they believe</u>: If you enter an angry person's vibratory field, those vibrations strike the "anger cells" in your brain and your entire being will vibrate at the anger frequency. Consequently, you will become irritated or angry.

What we know: Electrical impulses in the brain are generated both spontaneously and following stimulation. Mirror neurons reflect emotions such as anger observed in others. There are several brain areas that are more intimately involved in the emotion of anger. This is not frequency-dependent—no "anger frequency". Of the thousands of scientific studies, there is no evidence that neural oscillations or electroencephalographic activity are transmitted through the brain to other brains at a non-visible distance or have significant influences on anything besides brain and bodily function within an individual.

19. Thoughts attract

What they believe: Thought waves are magnetized and attract similar thoughts. The more forcefully you think about something, the stronger your thought waves will be.

What we know: There is no evidence for thought waves or magnetized thought waves. There is no correlation between how hard you think about something and what is emitted from your brain. The presence of mirror neurons helps explain the phenomenon of feeling what other people are experiencing. Mirror neurons fire similar patterns when we see someone express an emotion or behave in certain ways. Thought waves don't move between brains, but people in close proximity may still share similar neuronal patterns and exhibit similar emotions and feelings.

20. Magnetized thoughts

What they believe: Thoughts are magnetized fluid energy.

What we know: There is no known evidence that thoughts are magnetized. Nor are they fluid energy. Electromagnetic is different than magnetized in the traditional sense.

21. Negative thinking

What they believe: Negative thoughts and positive thoughts have different properties in terms of how they are sent from the brain and how the universe perceives them.

What we know: There is no evidence for any difference in negative or positive thoughts. The electroencephalogram (EEG), which measures electrical brain waves, is not able to detect differences between positive and negative thoughts. Lie detectors may pick up subtle difference in excitability with changes in frequency. Keep in mind that you can also learn how to "fool" this machine.

22. The universe knows

What they believe: The universe hears what you say and will give you more of the same. The universe only hears nouns, not adjectives or qualifiers. Therefore, don't use any negative words. Frame everything in terms of positives. Example: If you want to lose weight say, "I am thin" rather than "I want to lose weight." If you use the word "weight", the universe will give you more "weight".

What we know: There is **no** evidence or data that the universe is more concerned with nouns than your profound thoughts or deep-seated emotional desires. Some of the founders of the law of attraction used sentences with negative nouns and still claimed that they were able to achieve their goals. Has the law changed?

23. Universe creates pictures

<u>What they believe</u>: Law of attraction expert Jack Canfield states that the universe only sees pictures of your thoughts. That's why thoughts should be phrased only in the positive. "I'm tired of being poor." The universe creates a picture of poor and gives you more poor. However, he also states emotions are the consequences of thoughts. Feelings are more important than what you are saying.

<u>What we know</u>: It is unclear how these two sentiments can be reconciled. Yes, emotions are a true indicator of your thoughts. If the universe is intelligent and reflects my thoughts, why don't my true thoughts and feelings get reflected or "magnetized" instead of a select group of erroneous word-pictures that don't represent what I'm truly thinking or feeling? In my many years as a neuroscientist and researcher, I have found no known scientific evidence for the universe only being able to see "pictures" of thoughts.

24. Emotions over words.

<u>What they believe</u>: There are some law of attraction proponents who claim our words may not be that important. Thought is energy and emotion is an energy indicator. We broadcast our intentions all the time; verbal communication is inaccurate and less important. The power of attraction lies in "transmitting waves of emotion-based energy that resonates with similar emotional states in others."

<u>What we know</u>: It is true that our thoughts become emotions and are translated into words. The emotions are usually what we relate to. Obvious and intense emotions are perceived by others and reflected by similar neuronal firing patterns in their mirror neurons. This is

how like is reflected by like. In other words, yes, this is true and has nothing to do with energy levels or law of attraction.

25. Connecting minds

<u>What they believe</u>: Every mind and brain is connected to every other by way of the universal ether fluid and that it is not going to be too far into the future (from 1928) when everyone is going to be able to communicate by thoughts using the ether fluid. The flow continues forever in wavelengths, consistent with the intensity of the thought. This is why thoughts pop into your mind.

<u>What we know</u>: We are, as individuals, thinking beings. We have tens of thousands of thoughts every day, and complex lives. Spontaneous thoughts popping into our brains occur even in isolated individuals, enclosed behind windowless iron walls, or enclosed in large electromagnetic fields (like MRI machines), which would necessarily interfere with any kind of thought waves from other individuals. No one has yet tapped into the ether-mind communication web. There is zero evidence that wavelengths of any kind of energy correlate with thought intensity.

26. Mastermind

<u>What they believe</u>: When two or more minds come close enough together, the "mind stuff (electrons of the ether) mixes, sets up a chemical reaction, and initiates vibrations." This creates a third mind with similar thoughts—a "master mind."

<u>What we know</u>: Aside from Napoleon Hill's "feeling" that it must be like this, there is no scientific proof that any master mind exists.

27. *Formless stuff*

<u>What they believe</u>: Formless stuff (or Original Substance) is where everything is created. Formless stuff is intelligent and thinks. *Every* thought manifests as a form by being produced in the Formless stuff. The stuff permeates and fills the interspaces of the universe.

<u>What we know</u>: There is no proof of any intelligent Formless stuff that creates whatever we are thinking about. We each have about 60,000 to 80,000 thoughts per day (according to Deepak Chopra—although the origin of this number is difficult to find). There are about 7.2 billion people in the world. Therefore, the Formless stuff would start creating about 360 billion thoughts every minute or about 21.6 trillion thoughts per hour or about 500 trillion thoughts in 24 hours—that's 500,000,000,000,000 new things created by the Formless stuff every single day or 3½ quadrillion forms created in 7 days. That is one busy week! It's too bad that this "thinking" Formless stuff doesn't know when we are serious about the things we think. I'm thinking about a flying purple elephant that can do all of my housework and transport me to work—avoiding all of the traffic. Come on, Formless stuff, get to work!

Interestingly, Greg Kuhn[10] has postulated that the quantum field is the Formless stuff, since quantum mechanics suggests material things don't exist until we observe them. Quantum mechanics does not predict an "intelligent" quantum field, nor does it predict that our thoughts influence reality—merely that our presence may influence the outcome. In reality, it doesn't even predict that our presence is important, merely that some type of measuring device is present. Human will has nothing to do with this!

28. *Visualizing goals*

What they believe: When you visualize goals in the present tense, you vibrate more intensely for manifesting your image better. As Bob Proctor states, "You and energy particles move toward each other as dictated by the law of attraction."

What we know: Visualizing in the present tense may have more influence on your intentions. However, there is no evidence this technique has any influence on anything external to your person, such as universal energy particles. There is also no evidence you will vibrate more intensely when you visualize mindfully or that you will move toward energy particles as they move toward you.

29. *Manifesting*

What they believe: To manifest the visualization, you must stay focused on your goal and look at your board every day. In contrast, some modern day vision board experts state that simply creating the vision board is what is critical to maintaining the goal in your subconscious. You may be able to put it away and not look at it for years and still have the universe do the work for you.

What we know: All of your thoughts come from conscious or subconscious levels in your brain. If by having a thought it starts creating a form of my goal in the Formless stuff, then it should not matter whether or not I even make up a vision board. That thought is already in my subconscious and, according to law of attraction experts, floating around the universe and transmuting into my goal. How much time I spend looking at a board should not really be a factor, as long as I think about it at any point in time.

30. *Like attracts like*

<u>What they believe</u>: As in subatomic particles, like always attracts like. This is a basic and foundational premise of the law of attraction. It is a universal principal.

<u>What we know</u>: It is an incorrect assumption. In physics, like rarely attracts like. Opposites attract. By virtue of their existence, particles that have negative charges (like electrons) generate an electric field that exerts attractive forces on particles with positive charges (like protons). Electrons actually exert repulsive forces on other electrons—***like repels like***. Electrons can occupy the same orbit because of differing spins—not because of their charges. In fact, because they have similar charges, they cannot occupy the same space and are kept at a distance. This is a universal law. Law of attraction author Pam Grout[11] states that for every action there is an equal and *opposite* reaction. Yet she interprets this to mean you get back the same thing you send out. "If you criticize, you get criticized; if you lie, you'll be lied to." This is inconsistent with laws of electromagnetism and inconsistent with Newton's third law of motion.

31. *Quantum Field Theory*

<u>What they believe</u>: The universe is an unformed field of energy called the quantum field. The quantum field is a mass of energy with the potential to form everything you see in the material world.

<u>What we know</u>: Quantum mechanics describes the properties of subatomic particles; special relativity describes high-energy physics. Quantum field theory (QFT) is basically the extension of quantum mechanics in subatomic particles to fields, or larger systems of many

particles. QFT is one of the most difficult subjects in science and there are several concepts at this time, each with theoretical or mathematical limitations. QFT predicts new particles may appear or be destroyed, but how, when, and why this happens is not known. The most we can say is that the universe appears to have a baseline amount of energy. To extend the theory to one's individual thoughts is not justified.

32. *You create through thought*

<u>What they believe</u>: Quantum theory proves that we create our physical world by virtue of being an observer. The physical world does not exist until we observe it. Therefore, we create through thought. We choose the results of our observations.

<u>What we know:</u> There are some truths to this and some untrue suppositions. Quantum theory suggests that matter either exists as energy waves (where time and location don't matter) or as discrete particles. The electron is in a virtual state spread throughout space and does not have a specific location as a particle until being observed. For example, if I test to see if light is a wave, it is. If I test to see if light is a particle, it is. This is known as "wave collapse" since the act of observation collapses the infinite possibilities of where the electron will be into one discrete location.

So, how are they misinterpreting quantum theory? *First*, wave collapse is just one interpretation of quantum theory (Copenhagen interpretation). It is also possible that the observer could be split into different possibilities (Many-Worlds interpretation). *Second*, the observer in quantum mechanics does not have to be human or have a consciousness or a thought. Even a measuring device will be effective to collapse a wave. "Observer" is a technical term misused by law of attraction proponents. No one needs to pay attention to the results to influence the wave collapse into a single possibility. Third, quantum theory specifically deals with subatomic particles that are in many tiny places simultaneously. It does not apply to large objects. The macroscopic world is also influenced by gravity, general, and special relativity theories. Thinking that my neighbor's car will appear in my driveway is actually inconsistent with quantum theory, which would predict a small probability of it appearing in any given location.

33. Every cell has a consciousness

What they believe: Repressed emotions and memories are stored in cells throughout the body. All human cells are actually small units of consciousness and, as such, can collapse quantum possibilities.

What we know: This theory was set forth by Candace Pert,[12] an accomplished molecular biologist. She moved from neuropeptides being secreted from cells other than brain cells, to emotions are stored in cells, to all human cells are part of our consciousness. Unfortunately, the evidence is nil. She relied on speculation and huge theoretical leaps; postulating therapies based on massage and therapeutic touch would otherwise not trigger such profound transformations. She also erroneously associated consciousness with collapsing quantum waves, which is not a necessity.

It is interesting that several books, such as those by Greg Kuhn,[10] purport a scientific basis for the law of attraction, invoking quantum theory out of context. All science in favor of the theory is "proof". However, when scientific arguments are presented to the contrary, the comments become, "Science doesn't have all of the answers." Science is not a matter of selectively picking the data that supports your hypothesis. This amounts to outlandish, baseless speculation to support a preconceived idea. One must, with an open mind, consider and critique all reasonable evidence, continuously self-correcting a theory as competing hypotheses are tested.[13] To take unsubstantiated leaps of faith in science, when scientific evidence suggests otherwise, is limited to the dreamer. The critical thinker will wisely look elsewhere for answers.

Michael Shermer has identified twenty-five fallacies that lead people to believe weird things.[13] Here are a few thinking traps that he delineates: Using scientific language makes it science, anecdotes replace real evidence, bolder statements make it truer, rumors create reality, failures can always be rationalized, circular reasoning, ideological immunity, and problem-solving inadequacies (e.g. not seeking evidence to disprove the hypothesis).

Law of attraction proponents have created a "scientific" law (Like Always Attracts Like) and made several predictions based on that law (if I think about having a million dollars, I will get a million dollars). The evidence, it turns out, is the opposite of what was predicted by the law (no million dollars). Now they claim that the fact that it didn't happen supports their theory (you didn't do it well enough). Like any "bad" law, there is no way to ever scientifically disprove the law of attraction. Thus, I argue you should not dispel your belief simply because there is no law of attraction. Rather, eliminate your belief because it is detrimental to your health, wellness, and ability to achieve goals.

5

No Purpose

Vision board experts assert the principal reason the majority of vision boards fail is that their owners have not mastered techniques necessary to properly invoke the law of attraction. As a non-believer in the law of attraction, I think there are several explanations for vision boards failing. They are dreams without a purpose. In the book *E2*,[1] Pam Grout provides several examples of individuals who set their goals by asking the Infinite Potential, the Universe, God, or the "Infinite Dude" to give them some kind of sign regarding their purpose. Here's an example: "Hey dude, if it's true you have a plan for my life, I could use a directional pointer. I don't have a lot of time, so by Friday morning, I want to know just what you have in mind for me." How empowering! While your purpose may be divinely inspired, it should ultimately come from within you. This also explains why most New Year's resolutions fail to see goals brought to fruition.

Individuals creating vision boards are often told to cut out pictures of what they want to do, who they want to be, or what they want to have. They are focused on visualizing how this will look, feel, taste, and even sound. The focus is typically on manifesting a very specific desire—your deepest want. Typically, for vision boards, this involves material wealth or financial abundance. While vision boards may be used for other things as well, there is a long history of manifesting financial or material wealth and abundance.[2-6] The reason for setting money or material goods as goals is that many vision board and law of attraction experts believe that without material wealth it would be hard fulfilling other dreams and desires. Further material abundance will be able to complement your other goals so you can become "abundant" in other aspects of your life. In other words, you should attract money first and this will allow you to then attract other goals.

Many people are compelled to create a vision board after they read *The Secret* or see examples of vision boards. They are encouraged to include photos and pictures that specifically represent their goal. Why is this important? Your ability to achieve your goal is dependent only upon you and not the law of attraction. Thus, I attribute the lack of success with vision boards to a lack of motivation and direction toward the achievement phase of goal setting.

When people hear about the law of attraction, they gain an understanding that anything and any goal is possible. You are not limited by your strengths, lack of strengths, or reality. You are not limited by anything other than your own negative thoughts. If you can overcome this barrier, then with positive thoughts, emotions, and words, you may manifest whatever you desire. This is the question many vision board proponents ask of people wanting to create their own vision board: "You can achieve anything. What is it that you want? Be as specific as possible to let the universe know exactly and to get a very clear picture in your mind's eye." Proponents of vision boards correctly stress that you should let the pictures find you; the object of your desire should call out to you and you should, in turn, focus on attaining it with all of your intention.

It is in these instructions that the issue lies. It's about want; it's not about purpose. Vision boarders rarely ask themselves, "*Why* do I want this?" or "What is my motivation?" If your goal is to lose 50 pounds and you actually have to get off the couch to take some form of action to work out and cook healthy food, there is a lot of effort involved. It doesn't take long to realize this is difficult: the universe is not doing this for me and I have control over my own weight. I might not be that motivated to complete this task. It's easier to watch television. What's missing? A value-base to my goal.

By first doing a general self-assessment of your values, you can set goals that align with your deep-seated principles. This is what provides a burning motivation to become resilient and keep up the work when the going gets tough.

The best motivation to accomplish your goals is for the goals to have some deeper purpose or meaning. To maximize your motivation when you get tired and frustrated, base your purpose on your core values. This is often a missing step in vision boards; what Dr. Stephen Covey would call principle—or value—based goals.[6] Identify what it is about that goal that has deeper meaning to you. WHY do I care? Why do I want this? Why is this important to me? It is very rare to see this "why" on a vision board as the board is typically just pictorial.

Having your personal life mission and vision statement incorporated into a goal setting board converts your goal setting to a goal-achieving powerhouse. Having value-based goals is important in terms of manifesting whatever you want (more about this in Chapter 19). Let's take the example of wanting to lose 50 pounds:

I want to establish a goal. I know that I weigh too much and have thought about wanting to lose some weight for a while. I think, A vision board might be a great way to lose this weight. I can invoke the law of attraction and envision being thin. *Don't think,* I want to lose weight *or you'll get more weight. Don't think* I'm too fat *or you'll get more fat. Cut out pictures of thin people, models, Barbie, etc., motivating pictures that "speak" to you and represent exactly and specifically what you'd like to look like. Focus on these pictures and envision what it feels like and how it looks to be thin. Think of yourself as already being thin, what new clothes you'll wear, how great you'll look. Buy "thin" clothes and live life as if you're thin, in order to align your thoughts, emotions, and habits to really get the law of attraction working with you.*

What's missing from this discussion is the PURPOSE. Why do you want to lose weight? Why do you want to be thinner? When you are faced with your favorite chocolate cake, what is it that will stop you from having that second piece? The universe? Mental pictures of supermodels? No! That does not work. Let's look again at that goal of losing 50 pounds.

*I want to lose weight **because** my father was overweight and couldn't keep up with us as kids. He was not able to join us in activities and I really felt that we lost out from not having a better relationship with him. He died young from complications of diabetes due to being overweight. I value my relationship with my children and want to live long enough to be able to do things with them, not just to watch them grow up but to actively participate in their lives. This is what I need to focus on, the reason WHY this is important. Now when that chocolate cake appears in front of me, I have a deep-*

seated meaningful reason for not having that second piece. Heck, visualizing doing stuff with my kids, I may not even want that first piece of cake. I've started moving this goal "want" into a value-based "need".

Realize that in the first scenario I might have had the same values. But creating the vision board and utilizing the law of attraction did not necessitate my delving deeper into my purpose—my personal vision statement of who I want to be. Attaching a purpose to your goals converts your superficial desires into energizing passions.

6

No Action

Action is a complex subject in that it readily sparks heated debates among vision board enthusiasts. The present discussion applies specifically to vision boards invoking and enforcing the belief in the law of attraction. As reviewed earlier in this book, the law of attraction is based on the theory that like *always* attracts like. Negative thoughts, emotions, words, and actions attract more of the same. The most effective goals are established when there is alignment of your thoughts, emotions, words, and habits.

Thus, to truly activate the law of attraction and have the best chance at being able to use the power of the universe, vision board proponents strongly recommend you visualize yourself having already achieved your goal. Living as if you have already become, obtained, or accomplished your goal is the surest way to convince the universe you have faith in the law of attraction and that you have no doubts about your ability to attain this goal. What does it take to live like that? It takes a firm belief that you have already done what you want to do, become what you want to be and obtained what you want to have. Believers in the law of attraction will say that anything less is not going to yield positive results. You can't just pretend. You need to have your emotions in synch with your thoughts, beliefs, and actions. If your thoughts and beliefs are such that you've already attained your goal and then your actions suggest you aren't there yet, this is discordant. Discordance is negative. As it declares in *The Secret* that you need not take any action. Taking action suggests that you doubt the universe; a negative that will decrease your chance of success.

Once you have adopted the belief that you've already achieved your goal, it would be dishonest and insincere to take *any* action at all. After all, if you have already attained your goal, what action is there left to take? How can you realistically take action and still sincerely act as if you've already accomplished your goal? The answer is **you cannot**. If one is truly to believe in the law of attraction—that like *always* attracts like and you want your best chance of succeeding—then you should only have positive thoughts. Taking any action shows that you don't really believe that you have attained your goals. You've introduced doubt and thus negativity, a self-fulfilling negative cycle.

Law of attraction experts tell us the universe is caring; the universe is smart. Spending an hour per day visualizing that you have achieved your goal and then spending the rest of your day acting otherwise is disingenuous and negative. This behavior wouldn't fool a smart universe.

Here are quotes from law of attraction experts related to action:

- *"Think and speak of all the things you have asked for in terms of actual present ownership. Imagine an environment, and a financial condition exactly as you want them, and live all the time in that imaginary environment and financial condition."* (Wallace Wattles)

- *"There is no limit to what this law can do for you; dare to believe in your own ideal; think of the ideal as an already accomplished fact."* (Charles Haanel)

- *"When I walk in nature I'm in a state of joy. So I want to constantly put myself in that state, and when I do, then all I have to do is have the intention of what I want, and what I want manifests."* (Jack Canfield)
- *"Like Aladdin's Genie, the law of attraction grants our every command."* (Rhonda Byrne)
- *Believing involves acting, speaking, and thinking as though you have already received what you've asked for. When you emit the frequency of having received it, the law of attraction moves people, events, and circumstances for you to receive."* (Rhonda Byrne)
- *Receiving involves feeling the way you will feel once your desire has manifested."* (Rhonda Byrne)
- *"It takes no time for the Universe to manifest what you want. It is as easy to manifest one dollar as it is to manifest one million dollars."* (Rhonda Byrne)
- *"If you turn it over to the Universe, you will be surprised and dazzled by what is delivered to you. This is where magic and miracles happen."* (Dr. Joe Vitale)
- *"You are affirming this fact, believing that since you are thinking this, it is already yours."*[1] (Genevieve Behrend)
- *"The law of attraction then returns that reality to you, just as you saw it in your mind."* (Rhonda Byrne)
- *"Visualize checks in the mail"* to bring you more checks. (Rhonda Byrne)

- *Play games of having wealth and you will feel better about money; as you feel better about it, more will flow into your life."* (Rhonda Byrne)
- *"It's like having the Universe as your catalogue. You flip through it and say, 'I'd like to have this experience and I'd like to have that product and I'd like to have a person like that.' It is You placing your order with the Universe. It's really that easy."* (Dr. Joe Vitale)
- *"You can speed the creation of something simply by giving it more attention – the Law of Attraction takes care of the rest and brings to you the essence of the subject of your thought."* (Esther Hicks)
- *"You did not come into this environment to create through action."* (Esther Hicks)
- *"When you are better at applying your deliberate thought, there will not be so much action for you to tend to."* (Esther Hicks)

The above quotes are more typical of early days when the law of attraction was being introduced to the masses. Why are many vision board proponents now placing more importance on taking personal action to achieve goals and decreasing the glory of the law of attraction? Is it that the universe is becoming less powerful and less able to bring us what we truly, deeply want? With trillions of thoughts per week for the universe to deal with, is the universe overworked and underpaid? Are we becoming less "magnetized" and less able to attract what we think? No. The real answer is that law of attraction proponents are recommending action steps because there are so many dissatisfied vision boarders who have been relying on the universe to bring them the objects of their desires. This is why there are so many new books about the *secret to the secret, the key to the secret, the hidden, unknown secret to the secret, the clandestine techniques to manifesting the secret*, etc. What appeared initially to be such an easy way to achieve anything now seems so much more involved.

In *The Secret,* it is counterproductive to take action toward a goal. Taking an occasional "inspired action" is an exception to this rule. Inspired action is that which is derived from your "gut", "instinct", or "intuition", not conscious, logical planning. In contrast, Napoleon Hill wrote, "A leader who moves by guesswork, without practical, definite plans, is comparable to a ship without a rudder. Sooner or later he will land on the rocks."

In *The Secret,* John Assaraf describes how he was able to get his dream home through visualization and the law of attraction without any action (except for buying it). In *The Vision Board Book,*[2] *Assaraf* repeats this story and adds a chapter on Positive Action, where he suggests taking action is absolutely necessary to accomplishing your goal—you can't rely on the universe to get it for you. On his website, Assaraf's posts include, *"The Law of Attraction is not Enough to Achieve Your Goals,"* and *"Learn why the Law of Attraction Doesn't Work for Most People."* The law of attraction no longer does everything for you, it brings things toward you while you move toward the things that you want to achieve.

Dr. Srini Pillay, CEO of NeuroBusiness Group, describes the importance of *action* and visualizing *action* to invoke the law of attraction. Similarly, Joyce Schwarz of the Vision Board Institute also focuses on the importance of taking action. She even advertises her coaching program as helping others take action toward their goals. Her terminology now includes "co-creating" with the universe. I'm not sure how you can help others toward their goals unless the universe has inspired them to find you, to help them do this. Whatever happened to "our thoughts are things", "we create by our thoughts", "our thoughts manifest in the formless stuff to bring us our desired goals"?

Even *The Complete Idiot's Guide to Vision Boards*[3] suggests we don't just rely on the law of attraction. In fact, they not only suggest taking action, they emphasize, "…almost any action is good." It no longer needs to be inspired.

While I agree wholeheartedly with our need to take action, I want to emphasize that vision boards relying on the law of attraction should not also focus on *action steps*. Vision boards that claim the law of attraction is perfect and universal should be questioned when they say you are also required to take action. What action should you take if you've already accomplished your goal?

A conversation between a vision board coach (VBC) and me:

VBC: "Get into the right frame of mind and really live your life like you've already achieved your goal."

Farber: "Got it. This is incredible. I'm driving my new Maserati, living in my new 3 story, red brick house, sitting at my huge, granite desk in my new executive job, and spending my millions of dollars on more toys. Yes, I am living like I've done it. I've accomplished all of my goals and living the dream life… I've arrived!"

VBC: "Excellent. Now take some action and help the universe make that happen."

Farber: "I'm confused. What kind of action should I take? Why do I need to take any action? I just told you that I'm there already."

VBC: "The visualizing is great but now it's time to get serious and back to reality. You haven't really accomplished your goals yet. We were just pretending. Now you need to incorporate some action steps."

Farber: "I don't get it. I thought that visualizing was the key to success. I asked, I believed. Now don't I receive?"

VBC: "No, not yet. First you need to take action."

Farber: "Okay, what action steps do I take? It's hard to know since I feel like I've already got what I wanted."

VBC: "Well, you'll know when something comes to you after your visualization. It will be something inspirational to drive you toward your goal."

Farber: "How can something be inspirational to drive me to my goal from my visualization if I were successful at envisioning success already? I don't need inspiration because I've already accomplished it. Won't the universe know that I was just pretending?"

VBC: "Not if I don't tell the universe. I'll keep it a secret. Now get going and do something."

I find it interesting that ***every*** contributor to *The Secret* has taken actions to achieve success. Not one of them played a passive role and accomplished success through simply pretending their goals had already been realized. While they contributed to *The Secret*, they all focused on the power of the law of attraction—don't make plans; don't take action. Trust the universe. Think it and it will be delivered to you. Now that they each have their own followings, write their own books and are considered "experts", their tunes have changed. They now support the contention you *need* to take action to make your dreams come true; you can't rely on the universe. The law of attraction can't do it all. I applaud their openness to incorporate this concept, although this change came about through self-preservation, since the masses were realizing the law of attraction just wasn't taking care of business as promised. "There must be more to this," say the newfound "experts". They are right, there is more to this. The *law* of attraction does not exist. There is something better; something more effective, something that will lead to greater success and enhance your happiness and life satisfaction… You'll read about this in Chapter 19.

7

No Plan

If you believe in the law of attraction and you want to ASK, BELIEVE, AND RECEIVE to the best of your abilities, how can you best manifest your destiny? By living, breathing, feeling, and behaving as if your goals have already been realized. Recommendations vary amongst vision board experts as to the proper amount of time per day spent doing this idealized goal achievement visualization. Yet, all vision board proponents agree every thought is energy, all energy is "heard" or sensed by the universe, and that with every thought there is the creation of a product. The more intense your focus and concentration on the thought and goal, the faster and more likely you are to have your goal fulfilled.

Law of attraction experts, including Atkinson,[1] Wattles,[2] Hill,[3] and Mulford[4], made it sound ridiculously easy to achieve all of your goals by focused attention and thinking about them in a positive way. These recommendations made at the beginning of the New Thought Movement were more figurative than literal, as the original manuscripts focus on the importance of taking action and not relying on anyone else or the universe to do it for you. These authors were saying, "Don't limit yourself to what others think you are capable of. Dream big! You can achieve greatness if you believe in yourself.

Think positively and positive things will usually happen." Whether this was their goal or not, remains to be determined. What is true is that, in addition to taking action, authors like Napoleon Hill insisted that creating a plan was critical to becoming successful and implementing positive energy. In fact, Napoleon Hill describes six steps to turn "desire into gold." One of the essential steps is to create a definite, practical plan to accomplish your goal.

But when you believe you have already achieved your goal, why would you need to derive any kind of plan to attain it? How and why would you need to start thinking about formulating a plan? That doesn't make sense! You can't come up with a great plan if you believe you don't need one because you already have your goal.

In contrast to the originators of the law of attraction, modern-day "experts" like Hicks, Byrne, and all of the contributors to *The Secret* have emphasized you should never make a plan. By definition, inspired action is intuitive, does not come from a logical place, and therefore would not lend itself well to making any plans. Here are some quotes about planning from law of attraction experts:

- *"If you do just a little research, it is going to become evident to you that anyone that ever accomplished anything, did not know how they were going to do it."* (Bob Proctor)
- *"You don't need to know how it's going to come about. You don't need to know how the Universe will rearrange itself."* (Dr. Joe Vitale)
- *"How it will happen, how the Universe will bring it to you, is not your concern or job. Allow the Universe to do it for you. When you are trying to work out how it will happen, you are emitting a*

frequency that contains a lack of faith – that you don't believe you have it already. You think you have to do it and you do not believe the Universe will do it for you. The how is not your part in the Creative Process." (Rhonda Byrne)

- *"This is where magic and miracles happen."* (Dr. Joe Vitale)
- *"The 'hows' are the domain of the Universe. It always knows the shortest, quickest, fastest, most harmonious way between you and your dream."* (Mike Dooley)
- *"Our job is not to figure out the how." "...trust that the Universe will figure out how to manifest it."* (Jack Canfield)

It is interesting that these same authors now promote and sell **their** *"plans"* to help you achieve. When you read the research on goal setting and goal achieving, you'll find the overwhelming results show it helps to have a plan. It gives you direction and some insight as to possible challenges along the way.

It is obvious from reading dozens of books from law of attraction "experts" that it is no longer easy to get buckets of money and material abundance. We are asked to take a more active role in this process—to help the universe help us. The once powerful universe is not quite up to it anymore. We need to assist it. Check out Jack Canfield's website. It no longer states, *"Our job is not to figure out the how."* It now tells us that Jack can help you *"Learn to implement the keys to effective planning."* It says, *"Jack teaches that anyone can achieve their financial goals with effective planning..."* and *"...with Jack's guidance, you'll craft a plan for turning your goal into reality."* I agree, this is one of the ways Canfield and other successful individuals achieved their goals. Unfortunately, as shown in the discussion above, and as Byrne, Hicks, and the contributors to *The Secret* have stated, planning is difficult when you believe in and are true to the law of attraction.

Conversations between a vision board coach (VBC) and me.

Conversation #1

Farber: "My goal is to be a CEO in a big start-up company."

VBC: "Excellent. Try to visualize specifically what this will look like and how it will feel to be the CEO of this company."

Farber: "Wow, it feels amazing. All of the connections; all of the power. It is exactly what I thought it would feel like. I AM THE CEO!"

VBC: "That's great. Now let's come up with some plans to actually achieve this."

Farber: "What do you mean come up with some plans? I've already accomplished the goal. I AM THE CEO."

VBC: "No, I'm serious now, you aren't really the CEO yet. We were just pretending. You need to make some plans to get there."

Farber: "So much for that visualization!"

Conversation #2

Farber: "My goal is to be a CEO in a big start-up company."

VBC: "Excellent. Try to visualize specifically what this will look like and how it will feel to be the CEO of this company."

Farber: "Wow, it feels amazing. All of the connections; all of the power. It is exactly what I thought it would feel like. I AM THE CEO!"

VBC: "Okay, now just stay in that mindset and act like you've already achieved this position."

Farber: "I was told by someone at the bank that I might be eligible for a small business loan to get this idea off the ground. It sounds like a great start. There's only one issue."

VBC: "What's the issue?"

Farber: "The bank manager said that I will have to submit a business plan and you told me that any plans that I make will prevent me from achieving my goal. Making plans will involve identifying challenges, setting deadlines, acknowledging competition and setting up procedures. You said that doing these things would show the universe that I have doubt and then I'd never accomplish my goals."

Every successful venture needs a business plan. Without a business plan, you can't go to the bank for a business loan. A plan is your roadmap to success. This is not to say the plan can't or shouldn't change to accommodate ongoing needs, but, as Napoleon Hill emphasized, you need some kind of plan before you take action. He even has a chapter in *Think & Grow Rich*[4] called *"Organized Planning"* and states, "Millions of men go through life in misery and poverty, because they lack a sound plan through which to accumulate a fortune."

What will the bank say about my business loan request when my business plan simply states, "Waiting for this information from the universe"? Plans are critical to all goal achievement,[6] yet inconsistent with a true belief in the law of attraction; so sayeth Jack Canfield, Rhonda Byrne, Bob Proctor, Joe Vitale, et al.

8

No Date

Establishing deadlines is an essential component to the process of pursuing goals. Goal setting experts recommend formulating a completion date and even a timeline. Deadlines help steer our actions, focus our intentions, and motivate us to pursue our dreams with vitality.[1] Creating a deadline has been likened to drawing a line in the sand—a visible finish line. Deadlines help us budget our time appropriately and serve a role of keeping us productive and on track.

Deadlines are great for inspiring us to keep things moving forward and often challenge us to race against the clock when we set up "time goals" for ourselves. When used correctly, deadlines are wonderful tools that aid in seeing goals to fruition. They should be set with realistic guidelines. Otherwise, deadlines can be demotivating if we don't believe we have a chance to succeed. Without deadlines, many projects expand to fill space and time. Without a deadline there's always tomorrow. Deadlines tend to help us maintain our focus on what's important; decreasing the chance that we'll procrastinate. Goals without deadlines are just wishes. While your deadline remains in your head, it is just a whim. It attains power from being penned onto paper.

Obviously, is it extremely difficult to set deadlines when you are not the only one actively taking responsibility for accomplishing your goals. If you believe in the law of attraction and are asking the universe to help you then it will be impossible for you to set a deadline for the universe.

Vision board experts (correctly) encourage you to make your goals as specific as possible. Providing as much detail as you can helps make those goals come true. The proof is in the particulars; especially when you are visualizing the perfect outcome. Despite this, most vision board proponents recommend you don't set timeline goals. Never worry about time. Here are a few quotes about deadlines and time:

- *"Most of the time, when we don't see the things that we've requested, we get frustrated. We get disappointed. And we begin to become doubtful. The doubt brings about a feeling of disappointment."* (Rhonda Byrne)

- *"I don't have any rulebook that says it's going to take thirty minutes or three days or thirty days. It's more a matter of you being in alignment with the Universe itself."* (Joe Vitale)

- *"If you can understand that there is no time, and accept that concept, then you will see that whatever you want in the future already exists." "It takes no time for the Universe to manifest what you want."* (Rhonda Byrne)

- *"Don't worry if there are delays in manifestations...expect delays because there are still some signals blocking what you are trying to attract."* (Dr. Steve Jones)

- *"Often, delays in manifesting desires are not really delays. The Universe knows when to reflect signals back to its source. So when you want something, the Universe has to not only send what you asked for but it also has to modify existing circumstances to make the manifestation one hundred percent possible. So give the Universe some time..."* (Dr. Steve Jones)

Napoleon Hill, one of the grandfathers of the New Thought Movement, discussed the importance of having a **specific date** to achieve your goal. He wrote, "A goal is a dream with a deadline." While I agree with Napoleon Hill about the necessity of having a specific date and timeline for completing your goal, it is incongruent with a belief in the law of attraction. After all, why would I need a timeline to help me achieve my goal, when I've already achieved the goal? The book *The Secret*[2] takes care of this issue when it recommends you should never worry about time. This makes great sense. Why would you need a completion date if you've already done the task? How could you possibly set a timeline when you are not supposed to have any plans?

9

No Challenges

Positive and social psychology research has identified many benefits to encounter and plan for challenges. A healthy attitude towards challenges is associated with increased resilience and greater success. Viewing difficult situations as healthy challenges, rather than unwelcome problems, is what differentiates healthy and helpful stress from limiting and debilitating stress. Challenges are good. They allow us to rise up, use our strengths, and become empowered to succeed. Success guru Brian Tracy writes, "Only by contending with challenges that seem to be beyond your strength to handle at the moment you can grow more surely toward the stars."

With the right attitude, challenges don't paralyze you, they propel you to greatness. When you make realistic plans for the future, you identify potential challenges and start to come up with more definitive detailed plans of how you will rise to those challenges or, perhaps, under certain circumstances, avoid them. Every good business plan includes analysis of your competition, your strengths, opportunities, **weaknesses**, and ***threats.*** Acknowledging and dealing with realistic challenges is a formula for success!

"Okay", you say. "Why can't I incorporate obstacles and challenges into my vision board?" Great question! Because even talking about challenges and obstacles is an admission of doubt in the law of attraction. Identifying future or present challenges is considered a negative omen. If you truly believe in the law of attraction, you need to completely avoid any thoughts or discussions of potential, apparent, or even actual obstacles and challenges or you will attract more of the same into your life.

Here are some quotes about challenges from experts on vision boards and the law of attraction:

- *"Do not concern yourself with questions as to how you shall surmount obstacles which may loom upon your business horizon, unless you can see plainly that your course must be altered today in order to avoid them."* (Wallace Wattles)
- *"Nothing can come into your life without your attention to it."* (Esther Hicks)
- *"Once you have recognized that thinking of what you do not want only attracts more of what you do not want into your experience, controlling your thoughts will not be a difficult thing..."* (Esther Hicks)
- *"Good thoughts and actions can never produce bad results; bad thoughts and actions can never produce good results."* (James Allen)[1]
- *"The more steady and continuous your faith and purpose, the more rapidly you will get rich, because you will make only POSITIVE impressions upon Substance; and you will not neutralize or offset them by negative impressions."* (Wallace Wattles)[2]
- *"You must know that what you want is yours the moment you ask.*

You must have complete and utter faith." (Lisa Nichols)
- *"Ask once, believe you have received, and all you have to do to receive is feel good."* (Rhonda Byrne)
- *"...trust that the Universe will figure out how to manifest it."* (Jack Canfield)
- *"The Universe will start to rearrange itself to make it happen for you."* (Dr. Joe Vitale)

If the law of attraction requires you live as if your goals have been completed, then you should never contemplate the possibility of any obstacles. This is considered negative. Admittedly, many early writers of the New Thought Movement viewed challenges and even failures as being beneficial. But, as with taking action, making plans, and setting timelines, it is inconsistent and unnecessary to contemplate challenges if you've already achieved what you want. Intently visualizing and living as though your dreams have been realized makes it impossible to contemplate future potential obstacles or acknowledge present challenges.

Avoiding all obstacles and challenges is unrealistic. If you don't look at and plan for potential obstacles, you will be unprepared mentally, emotionally, and practically for facing real challenges when they arise.

10

No Compassion

Implicit in a belief in the law of attraction is the conviction that you should not have sympathy or empathy for those less fortunate than yourself. This may seem harsh, yet it is a direct result of believing that like *always* attracts like and that the universe will give you whatever it is that you are thinking about.

Wallace Wattles, one of the founders of the law of attraction, whose writings formed some of the basis for *The Secret*, instructs that people are only poor because of their poor thoughts. Helping them will only increase your chances of becoming poor. Since you don't want to attract any negativity, do not give any money to the poor or help anyone in poverty.

Here are some quotes from law of attraction expert Wallace Wattles[1] on compassion and helping others:

- *"Do not talk about poverty; do not investigate it, or concern yourself with it. Do not spend your time in charitable work, or charity movements, all charity only tends to perpetuate the wretchedness it aims to eradicate."*

- *"Do not read books or papers which give circumstantial accounts of the wretchedness of the tenement dwellers, of the horrors of child labor, and so on. Do not read anything which fills your mind with gloomy images of want and suffering. The* poor do not need charity; they need inspiration. No matter how horrible in seeming may be the conditions in certain countries, sections, or places, you waste your time and destroy your own chances by considering them. Give your attention wholly to riches; ignore poverty."

- "It is the desire of God that you should get rich." "Get rid of the idea that God wants you to sacrifice yourself for others, and that you can secure his favor by doing so; God requires nothing of the kind."

Similarly, if you believe like *always* attracts like, then you will want to avoid thinking about, looking at, or interacting with anyone who is physically, psychologically, emotionally, or spiritually unwell. Anyone less well than yourself should be avoided. Law of attraction supporters suggest that you should not talk to anyone about their illnesses or health issues because it will bring sickness into your life.

Rhonda Byrne, in *The Secret*, even goes so far as to write:

"If you see people who are overweight, do not observe them... If you think or talk about diseases, you will become sick. If you think or talk about psychological or emotional problems, you will become psychologically or emotionally unhealthy. If you think or talk about poverty, you will become poor. What you think or surround yourself with – good or bad, is what you will bring upon yourself."

Also, from *The Secret*,

"You are also inviting illness if you are listening to people talking about their illness. As you listen you are giving all of your thought and focus to illness, and when you give all of your thought to *something, you are asking for it. And you are certainly not helping them. You are adding energy to their illness."*

I am not making this up. While it may seem crazy, if you truly believed in the law of attraction, you would never surround yourself with people who have physical illnesses or diseases. Thus, you should avoid being in or interacting with anyone in the following professions:
- Physician
- Nurse
- Dentist
- Chiropractor
- Podiatrist
- Physician Assistant
- Nursing Assistant
- Any other form of healthcare professional
- Anyone who works in a hospital: secretarial, administrative, engineering, service or maintenance worker
- Also, don't visit any sick or hospitalized friend or family member

Just as outrageous, if you truly believed in the law of attraction, you would never surround yourself with people who have mental, psychological, or emotional issues or anyone who discusses the emotional hardships in their lives. Thus, you should avoid the following professions:
- Rabbi
- Priest
- Pastor
- Any other clergy member
- Psychiatrist
- Psychologist

- Social worker
- Coach
- Counselor
- Any other type of therapist

Still more craziness, if you truly believed in the law of attraction, you would never surround yourself with people who have financial hardships. Thus, you should avoid the following professions:
- Accountant
- Mortgage broker
- Banker
- Lawyer
- Loan officers

Not done yet. If you are a believer and have in the law of attraction you would never associate with or be near people who get injured. Thus, you should avoid the following professions:
- Police
- Firefighter
- Paramedic
- Any military career

Remember, if you truly believe in the law of attraction, you should **never volunteer for any charity or donate to a charity**. If there exists a law of attraction, anyone in any of the above professions would be less healthy, less wealthy, and less satisfied with life.

Moreover, if there were a law of attraction, expect all personal trainers to be overweight and out-of-shape. Indeed, Jillian Michaels, the highly toned fitness coach from the television show *The Biggest Loser*, would be obese and unhealthy by now! As Wallace Wattles states, "*Medicine as a science of disease has increased disease; religion as a science of sin has promoted sin, and economics as a study of poverty will fill the world with wretchedness and want.*"

Can these statements be true? Obviously not, which is one of the reasons there cannot be a law of attraction. I am a physician treating sick people. I regularly volunteer on medical missions to help the needy. I coach people with emotional issues and I'm a personal trainer and martial arts instructor to improve others' physical health and well-being. These activities do not make me sick; they improve my health and happiness.

Many research studies also dispute this law of attraction prediction. They show that altruistic people are healthier and happier.[1,2] Helping people increases oxytocin levels and this correlates with happiness and life satisfaction. In contrast to the predictions of the law of attraction, helping those in need has been proven to enhance your own health.

Here's another interesting fact. Through my investigations, I found I am not the only one who does not believe in the predictions of the law of attraction. *All contributors* to the book *The Secret*[3] are indeed generous to those less fortunate and have all contributed to charities; some even started their own organizations to help the needy. While I applaud and commend this altruistic behavior, we should realize it does go against the law of attraction.

11

No Support

Vision board experts tell us it doesn't matter whether or not you believe in the law of attraction. It's a universal law that works whether or not you have faith in it. But it's not that easy. There are many more secrets and keys and missing links to explain why the success rate, even for firm believers and practitioners, is so low. What this means is that you've got to set your thoughts, feelings, habits, and actions all in alignment with your desired goal. As John Assaraf puts it, you need to bring your conscious and subconscious mind into alliance. What does that mean in real terms? It means that a true belief in the law of attraction would severely limit your employment opportunities and the kinds of jobs and careers in which you should be involved. Are there other consequences of a belief in the law of attraction? YES, there are! Please read on.

As shown in the last chapter, being empathetic and compassionate goes against the law of attraction. Moreover, since this law dictates that like *always* attracts like, needing to always surround yourself with happy, healthy, and successful individuals has additional implications. You should not be around, associate with, or seek help from people with illnesses, diseases, sicknesses, and other issues related to poor habits or poor health.

Support groups are comprised of like-minded individuals, sharing stories and experiences. They help people realize that they're not alone. They are effective in guiding those with similar interests and health issues to incorporate successful strategies. Yet, according to *The Secret*, if you are trying to lose weight you should avoid looking at or interacting with people who are overweight. In other words, support groups would be dangerous and counterproductive to attaining your goals. If you believe in the law of attraction, avoid these groups at all costs:

- Alcoholics Anonymous
- Weight Watchers
- Tough Love Parenting
- Diabetes Support
- Cardiac Support groups
- Divorce Support groups
- Post-traumatic Stress Support
- Phobia Support Groups
- Stress Relief Groups
- Bulimia Support
- OCD Support
- Breast Cancer Support
- Alzheimer's Support
- AIDS Support
- Grief Support
- Gamblers Anonymous
- Sexual Abuse Survivors
- Debtors Anonymous
- Fibromyalgia Support Group
- Stroke Groups
- Suicide Prevention
- Asperger's Syndrome Support
- Brain Trauma Support
- Families of Addicts/Alcoholics
- Infertility Groups
- Victims of Domestic Violence
- Eating Disorders
- Any types of group therapy
- Any other support group for physical or mental conditions.

The law of attraction predicts these support groups would worsen, rather than alleviate, any symptoms. However, this is not the case. If you are facing major life changes or serious health issues, *support* groups do just that. They show you that you are not alone in your journey. Support groups have great health and wellness benefits[1,2] including: feeling less isolated or judged, improving your coping skills, gaining a sense of control, the ability to speak openly about what you're dealing with, reducing depression and anxiety, sharing and learning practical advice and information from others in similar situations, and being able to compare notes about treatment options and resources. It's too bad that the law of attraction doesn't recommend participating in one of these groups. Alcoholics Anonymous and Weight Watchers are two groups that have shown to be of great benefit for their members. Anyone who has watched the television show *The Biggest Loser* has witnessed the enhanced motivation and successful weight loss results occurring in this group format.

12

Mindless

Visualization is key to vision boards and the law of attraction. The principle behind creative visualization is that you live your life as if your goal had already been realized (see Chapter 2). Let's look at visualization in more detail.

1) Why visualize? Because like *always* attracts like. This means if you visualize yourself as having achieved your goal in the present tense, you will send this frequency to the universe and be rewarded with a matching frequency. You will attract more of the same. The universe will create this situation for you from the Formless Substance.

2) What should you visualize? Visualize your perfect outcome. To attract perfect, you must visualize perfect. The universe is not stupid. It knows if you've been bad or good, so be good for goodness' sake. Have no doubts about your success. Don't just pretend; the universe won't stand for that. It will detect insincerity and it will give you back more of the same.

3) When should you visualize? This is an interesting question. The purpose of visualizing is three-fold. First, it helps you clarify your goal and picture yourself living as if you've obtained or become exactly what you have dreamed of, living and feeling all of the details of what that life will be like. Second, it brings you to a place in which you are completely enveloped by the feeling of

accomplishment of your dream, a positive feeling to attract more positivity. Third, while you live a life of fulfillment, you will not be having any doubts or negativity that will inevitably slip in while you are living your normal daily life. Visualizing a future state in the present tense helps you escape the harsh realities of today.

Why did I say that this was an interesting question? Because as there have been so many dissatisfied law of attraction customers, the experts (including Joyce Schwarz and John Assaraf) now suggest you only visualize for a short time each day and then come back to reality in order to take action. The "all powerful" law of attraction as described by the Hicks'[1] and in *The Secret*[2] is no longer able to do this job without you taking physical action. So the compromise is to pretend only for a little while and then go about trying to make it happen.

You can accept this method blindly or look at it with serious discernment. If 1) the universe is so powerful that it can create an endless supply of everything that I want, 2) the best way to get it is to have complete, focused attention and awareness on the object of my desire, and 3) any negative has the real chance of completely ruining my ability to attain this goal ... then why wouldn't I want to visualize this outcome all day long until it happens? To do otherwise makes sense only if you don't believe in the awesomeness of the law of attraction and your power to create by your thoughts.

Now let's take a closer look at what you are supposed to visualize. *Outcome*. Visualize that you have achieved your goal. Here are some quotes about outcome visualization from law of attraction experts:

- *"Believe that it is already yours. Have what I love to call unwavering faith."* (Lisa Nichols)

- *"See the things that you want as already yours. Think of them as yours, as belonging to you, as already in your possession."* (Robert Collier)

- *"You must act, speak, and think, as though you are receiving it now. If your thoughts contain noticing you do not have it yet, you will continue to attract not having it yet. You have to emit the frequency of having received it, to bring those pictures back as your life. When you book a vacation, order a brand new car, or buy a house, you know those things are yours. You wouldn't go and book another vacation for the same time, or purchase another car or house. If you won a lottery or received a large inheritance, even before you physically had the money, you know it is yours. That is the feeling of believing it is yours."* (Rhonda Byrne)

- *"If you turn it over to the Universe, you will be surprised and dazzled by what is delivered to you. This is where the magic and miracles happen."* (Dr. Joe Vitale)

- *"Do whatever you have to do to generate the feelings of having it now, and remember them. Not 'I wish I could get that car,' or, 'Some day I'll have that car,' because that's a very definite feeling associated with that. It's not in the now. It's in the future. If you stay in that feeling, it will always be in the future."* (Bob Doyle)

- *"Trust the Universe. Trust and believe and have faith. You must imagine, pretend, act as if, make-believe, that the perfect weight is yours."* (Rhonda Byrne)

- *"When you're visualizing, when you've got that picture playing out in your mind, always and only dwell upon the end result."* (Mike Dooley)
- *"You are also implementing trust and faith in the Universe, because you are focusing on the end result and experiencing the feeling of that, without giving any attention whatsoever to 'how' it will come about."* (Rhonda Byrne)
- *"Fast-forward to the happy end results that you are seeking. Imagine already having achieved whatever it is that you desire."* (Esther Hicks)[1]

Visualizing outcome over process and envisioning the future as if it has already occurred means you are not living mindfully in the present. Believers in the law of attraction will comment that you are being mindful in that you are truly living *as if* the future is occurring in the present. Yes, this is true, but you are missing out on the reality of what's around you right now!

The positive power of mindfulness in lowering stress, decreasing depression, improving immunity, and enhancing life satisfaction is mitigated when you spend your time dreaming about the future—even when you pretend or imagine that the future is right now. Eckert Tolle's book, *The Power of Now*,[3] describes how great it is to be mindful and live in the present. It doesn't say live in the future and pretend that is now. In another law of attraction book, *E2*, Pam Grout[4] recommends staying focused on your future goal, despite the "menacing distractions" such as your present situation that will arise. This is not being mindfully present or positive.

There are several important studies showing that mentally

simulating (envisioning) an outcome (living in the future) often results in less success and may even be detrimental. It is better to visualize a process—a golf swing, how you are going to study for an exam, how and where you will apply for jobs—than visualize winning a tournament, getting an "A" on an exam, or having a beautiful office.

Envisioning the perfect outcome as if it already happened DECREASES YOUR CHANCE OF SUCCESS. This is not an opinion; this is based on excellent psychology research in mental simulations (visualizations). Whether you are talking about jobs, academic achievement, health issues, or weight loss, *more positive fantasy outcomes of a desired future predict less success at achieving goals.*[5,6]

Here are a few examples:

- Golfers, tennis pros, figure skaters, basketball players, and Olympic athletes who visualize themselves winning a big tournament, embodying what it feels like standing on the podium, holding the trophy and the media taking pictures, will not do as well or try as hard as those who picture exactly how and where they were going to train, envisioning the realistic challenges along the way, and the process of how they will compete.[7-11]
- College students: Group 1 spent a few minutes each day visualizing how great it would feel to make a high grade on an important exam. Group 2 spent a few minutes each day picturing when, where, and how they intended to study. The first (outcome) group studied less and made lower grades on the exam. They achieved less. Students envisioning studying and

planning (process) prepared better, studied more, scored higher grades and were less stressed.[6]
- College graduates who visualized getting their dream job after college submitted fewer job applications, received fewer job offers, and had lower salaries than those who visualized *how* they were going to look for their jobs.[6]
- Highly competitive skiers were more successful if they used task (process) visualizations and considered performance challenges compared to those who relied simply on positive thinking.[12]
- College students who had romantic crushes were less likely to be successful at establishing a relationship with that person if they had more positive fantasies about the relationship.[5]

Visualization experts Shelley Taylor and Lien Pham argue, "...*mental simulation of the **process** for reaching a goal or of the **dynamics** of an unfolding stressful event produced progress in achieving those goals or resolving those events. Envisioning successful **completion** of a goal or resolution of a stressor—recommendations derived from the self-help literature **did not**.*"[13,14]

Vision board proponents point toward athletes as evidence for the power of visualization. Yes, many successful athletes use visualization for achieving great feats and even gaining strength in their sport. Research shows that using mental imagery activates brain areas in the motor cortex, allowing the body to become stronger simply through brain activation without even lifting a muscle.[15] This is process visualization—how to train, not the outcome of standing with a medal.

There are also multiple examples, both personal and in well-controlled scientific studies, of patients who have accelerated the healing process through visualization. One such study shows mental imagery helping victims of childhood abuse, improving their self-esteem and decreasing post-traumatic stress.[16] This occurs by visualizing the *process* of skin shedding, not by visualizing a positive outcome. Furthermore, research shows that *process* visualization helps obese women lose weight. When women in weight loss programs use *outcome* visualization (as recommended by vision board experts) they actually gain weight!

Why would this happen? The answer is so clear that before we go to the scientific literature to show why futuristic idealist visualization is a poor choice, let's look to the law of attraction experts for the answer.

- *"This is such a holographic experience – so real in this moment – that you don't even feel as if you need the car, because it feels like you have it already."* (Dr. Joe Vitale)
- *"That's why you don't feel as if you need it anymore, because you tuned in and felt the real field of creation through your visualization."* (Rhonda Byrne)
- *"Your picture in your mind is seeing it as done. Your feelings are seeing it as done. Your mind and your entire state of being are seeing it as already happened. That is the art of visualization. If you had placed an order from a catalogue you would relax, know you are going to receive what you ordered, and get on with your life."* (Rhonda Byrne)

This last quote drives home the message and confirms what research scientists have known for some time. Visualizing ideal futuristic goals being attained saps your energy and decreases your motivation to play an active role. Multiple studies have shown that when people are fantasizing they've already achieved their goals, their blood pressure, energy levels, and motivation hit an all time low.[17] They have succeeded in fooling themselves into believing they've accomplished their goals. If you've already achieved success, you don't need to concern yourself with the process. That's what law of attraction experts told them to do. Unfortunately, they now have less motivation to plan and act toward actually realizing their goal. They'd better hope the universe steps up to the plate!

Being fully engaged in and appreciating the process is the road to mindfulness. While vision board experts continue to discuss the importance of visualization, most of them are using the wrong set of visualization images to help achieve goals. While debating this topic with Joyce Schwarz, author of *The Vision Board*,[18] she gave me the following examples of the benefits of "outcome" visualization. Remember, I'm a proponent of visualization, but it has to be the right type (as seen in Chapter 19). Unfortunately, none of her examples actually showed any benefit to successful outcome visualization. I am including a brief synopsis of each and the reference so that you can read them for yourselves.

1) *Picture elicitation*: This article is an overview of the benefits of using imagery and plasma screen distractions to enhance the healing of various medical conditions like post-traumatic stress disorder. I agree this is a great use of visualizations. This is NOT visualization of a successful outcome. (psychologytoday.com/ blog/design-my-mind/201104/healing-imagery-the-brains-own-natural-bag-visual-tricks)

2) *Symbology:* (*Man and His Symbols* by Carl Jung). This is a great book from a leader in psychology. The book describes Jungian philosophy about the unconscious, dreams, archetypal characters, extraversion and introversion, religion, good and evil, and much more. It does NOT address visualization of successful outcomes.

3) *Archetypes:* Ms. Schwarz refers me to a Wikipedia article on Jungian archetypes and mental imagery. Jungian theory of archetypes focuses on the collective unconscious and does NOT address benefits of outcome visualization. (Wikipedia.org/wiki/Jungian_archetypes)

4) *Mental Imagery*: Schwarz refers to a book called *The Case for Mental Imagery* by Kosslyn, Thompson, and Ganis. They describe the history of mental simulations and focus on propositional versus depictive representations. This is an interesting academic discussion that does NOT address visualization of successful outcomes. (books.google.com/books/about/The_Case_for_Mental_Imagery.html?id=...)

5) *Mental Simulation*: Interesting article confirming process-driven visualizations (aka Action Board-type)—athletes visualizing running and students visualizing how they will study are better than outcome-driven visualizations (aka vision board-type). (Psychologicalscience.org/index.php/news/releases/mental-simulations-of-social-thought-and-action.html)

6) *Word Association*: This article supports my visualization techniques of process over outcome. Athletes improve strength simply by visualizing movements. There was no advantage to visualizing that they were strong and successful at lifting

weights—again, in this setting, no benefit to outcome visualization. (psychologytoday.com/blog/bodysense/201109/strength-training-using-motor-imagery)

7) *Attentional Focus:* Great article demonstrating benefits of process-driven visualizations. Athletes imagining their biceps moving had more success, greater achievements, and more EMG activity than if they imagined that the bar was moving during pull-ups. (athleticinsight.com/Vol10Iss2/MuscularActivity.htm)

8) *Lucid dreaming*: This article discusses REM sleep, mood disorders, Freudian theories, medications affecting dreaming, and manipulating dreams during sleep (lucid dreaming). How this article relates to outcome visualizations is unclear. (psychologytoday.com/blog/sleeping-angels/200905/why-we-dream-and-what-happens-when-we-do)

9) Color Psychodynamics: This article describes the effects of different colors in the environment on psychophysiological and behavioral reactions of severely delayed children. 1) Light simulating sunshine was better than fluorescent lighting. 2) Aggressive behaviors were more frequent in the afternoon while destructive behaviors occurred more often in the morning. I refer you to Joyce Schwarz for how this relates to outcome visualization. (eric.ed.gov/?id=ED216468)

10) *Mental Cleansing*: Great article about how psychologists used visualizations to successfully treat victims of childhood sexual abuse and improve their post-traumatic stress. Participants learned about how often their skin cells had been "shed" since their last contact with their abusers and then visualized shedding

their contaminated skin. Victims succeeded through visualizing the process of skin shedding, not by visualizing the outcome of being whole. (scientificamerican.com/article.cfm?id=mental-cleansing)

11) *Immersive simulation*: *Environmental Psychology* study shows when college students are walking in nature or imagining that they're walking in nature, they have more energy and feel more alive. (sciencedaily.com/releases/2010/06/100603172219.htm)

In summary, when you focus on the *outcome* and not the *process*, you live the future. You are bringing the future to the present, a mindless disrespect for the power of now. I am a believer in the power of visualization. Yet all visualization is not considered equal. The most powerful visualization methods have been incorporated into the Principle of DIVINE visualization (discussed later in this book). This is not based on personal opinion but on mind-brain science and ground-breaking research. I have personally used these techniques to successfully recover from spinal cord trauma (twice) and back surgeries (where I was told that I may not walk again without a cane) and previously debilitating arthritis. I am back to being able to do the splits, diving rolls, back flips on a trampoline, walk for 25 miles and actively teach martial arts!

13

Blame Yourself

Proponents of the law of attraction believe this law is absolute and perfect – like the law of gravity. Whether you believe in it or not, as a universal law it can have no flaws; make no mistakes. Remember, like *always* attracts like. We act like magnets, attracting whatever we send out to the universe. Thoughts are energy and as soon as we think of our goal, it starts being manifested. All we need to do is be positive and open to receive these gifts.

If this theory is true, then realistically you should get everything you've ever hoped for or dreamt about. Obviously, this has not happened. Even those who have studied the law of attraction, are avid practitioners of "the law" and who have created exotic vision boards are still unsuccessful at achieving their goals. Why is this so? There are two possible explanations. Either there is no law of attraction, or you are not properly invoking the law and using it to your benefit. This means that if you are unsuccessful at accomplishing your goal, **you are to blame.**

Here are some quotes from law of attraction experts about individual responsibilities:

- *"The only reason why people do not have what they want is because they are thinking more about what they don't want than what they want. Like all the laws of nature, there is utter perfection in this law."* (Rhonda Byrne)

- *"Nothing can come into your experience unless you summon it through persistent thoughts. You are the one who calls the law of attraction into action, and you do it through your thoughts."* (Rhonda Byrne)
- *"You become what you think about most, but also attract what you think about most."* (John Assaraf)
- *"It's as easy to create a castle as a button."* (Esther Hicks)
- *"If you can think about what you want in your mind, and make that your dominant thought, you **will** bring it into your life."* (Rhonda Byrne)
- *"See yourself living in abundance and you will attract it. It works every time, with every person."* (Bob Proctor)
- *Here's the problem. Most people are thinking about what they don't want, and they're wondering why it shows up over and over again."* (John Assaraf)
- *"Your thoughts and feelings create your life. It will always be that way. Guaranteed!"* (Lisa Nichols)
- *"I'd like to have this experience and I'd like to have that product and I'd like to have a person like that. It is You placing your order with the Universe. It's really that easy."* (Dr. Joe Vitale)
- *"...if you stay focused on the positive things in your life, you will automatically attract more good and positive things into your life. If you are focused upon lack and negativity, then that is what will be attracted into your life."* (Jack Canfield)

- *"Realization of your wish is accomplished by assuming the feeling of the wish fulfilled. You cannot fail unless you fail to convince yourself of the reality of your wish."* (Neville Goddard)[1]
- *"...it is impossible to experience the absence of something desired if your beliefs about that desired thing are truly positive. So, if you are experiencing an absence of a desired outcome, your true, underlying beliefs about that thing must be negative. If they were truly positive, you would already be experiencing that desired outcome right now."* (Greg Kuhn)[2]
- *"Without exception, that which you give thought to is that which you begin to invite into your experience. You get the essence of what you are thinking about, whether it is something that you want or something that you do not want."* (Esther Hicks)[3]
- *"...if you're not getting the answers you want, that's not the field of potentiality's fault. It's you that's screwing up the principle."* (Pam Grout)[4]

What is the end result of this belief? If you are unsuccessful in attaining your goal, it is because you introduced some negativity or doubt. Thus, as vision board coaches have explained to me, if your vision board is not successful, it's your fault!

Vision board enthusiasts believe that our thoughts are vibrations and these vibrations are not fixed. One can change their vibrations by modifying what they are saying, thinking, and feeling. If you want to bring in more wealth, yet mention being broke, the universe will hear you focus on being broke and send you more of the same. You will be responsible for keeping yourself in this situation.

As a proponent of being accountable, we are each responsible for our thoughts, feelings, actions, and reactions. However, as Dr. Stephen Covey conveyed,[5] we are not responsible for the actions or thoughts of others. In contrast, Napoleon Hill and other law of attraction experts believe our thoughts have profound effects on others; my thoughts do not control anyone else's actions.

Believing you are in control of *all* facets of your life (including natural phenomena and other people's thoughts and actions) results in lowered self-esteem and excessive self-blame. It decreases the ability to problem-solve, learn from the lack of success, and move toward a better solution. Jack Canfield dedicated much of his career to helping people become more responsible for their lives. In *The Secret*, he writes, *"Our job is not to figure out the how."* This is certainly not a statement of responsibility.

Vision board expert John Assaraf wrote about an unsuccessful visualization that he had when he was a teenager.[6]

"...I wanted more than anything in the world to be a basketball star. I wanted this so badly that I used to imagine myself making those winning shots that won championship games. When I went to sleep at night, there was a basketball beside me under the covers. I held onto my vision literally, day and night."

It sounds like he did everything correctly. So, did he become a basketball star? No. Why wasn't his visualization successful? Rather than assuming responsibility, which he should do as a believer in the law of attraction, Assaraf takes a different approach. First, he blames a "near-fatal car accident" which cut his dream short. Next, he claims that his goal was sort of fulfilled because he used that same drive and determination to achieve other goals. He negates the fact that, according to the law of attraction, he is the one who caused the car accident.

There may be reasons, other than incompetence, why your goal is not attained. You may have achieved 90% of your goal and deserve to reward, not blame yourself for failure. Two or more people may have the same vision and only one person can achieve a goal—winning a race or owning a specific house. The law of attraction suggests that more than one person could win a race or buy the same house, there are no limitations—anything is possible. That is fantasy, not reality. Perhaps God or the universe has other plans for you and this is really a blessing in disguise. For the person or people not achieving their goal, rather than self-blame, time would be better spent looking for reasons for the lack of success, changing course, demonstrating resilience, coming up with new plans, and again taking action.

As explained previously, Rhonda Byrne and Esther Hicks had contract disputes. While they could compromise and try to come up with mutually agreeable solutions, they would not both be getting exactly what they were asking of the universe. When Esther Hicks lost out, she commented that Abraham told her this would be for the better. I agree it is healthier to look for blessings in disguise. Unfortunately, this is not what they tell others who make up their own vision boards.

14

Blame the Victim

According to the law of attraction, everything someone experiences is their fault; good or bad. Since like *always* attracts like, if someone has a disease, illness, or accident, they brought it upon themselves. If someone suffers, it is by virtue of his or her own dysfunctional thoughts and feelings.

Here are some quotes about personal control and fault from law of attraction experts:

- *"...the condition of being overweight was created through your thought to it. To put it in the most basic terms, if someone is overweight, it came from thinking 'fat thoughts,' whether that person was aware of it or not. A person cannot think 'thin thoughts' and be fat.* **It completely defies the law of attraction.** *Whether people have been told they have a slow thyroid, a slow metabolism, or their body size is hereditary, these are all disguises for thinking 'fat thoughts'. Think perfect thoughts and the result must be perfect weight. Food cannot cause you to put on weight, unless you think it can."* (Rhonda Byrne)
- *"If you feel fat, you cannot attract thin."* (Esther Hicks)
- *"...it is a known fact that a person who has a vitalized brain is practically, if not entirely immune from all manner of disease."* (Esther Hicks)

- *"Every individual creates every aspect of their experience - we are in complete control of our health throughout our entire lives. There are no accidents."* (Esther Hicks)
- *"Disease cannot live in a body that's in a healthy emotional state."* (Bob Proctor)
- *"Am I saying that you are responsible for all your troubles, your suffering, and the absence of your desires? I suppose that's one way someone could choose to view it...I am not claiming that people in horrific circumstances, like abused children, are responsible for their circumstances. I have no explanation for abusive situations like this..."* (Greg Kuhn)[1]
- *"You can change your life and you can heal yourself."* (Michael Bernard Beckwith)
- *"You cannot 'catch' anything unless you think you can, and thinking you can is inviting it to you with your thought."* (From The Secret)
- *"Good thoughts and actions can never produce bad results; bad thoughts and actions can never produce good results. Suffering is always the effect of wrong thought in some direction. Disease and health, like circumstances, are rooted in thought."* (James Allen)[2]
- *"Both poverty and riches are the offspring of thought."* (Napoleon Hill)
- *"To look upon the appearance of disease will produce the form of disease in your own mind, and ultimately in your body, unless you hold the thought of the truth, which is that there is no disease; it is only an appearance, and the reality is health. The

thoughts of disease produce the forms of disease." (Wallace Wattles)[3]

- *"...there is no drug which has within itself the power to heal disease. If man will think only thoughts of perfect health, he can cause within himself the functioning of perfect health..."* (Wallace Wattles)[2]

Napoleon Hill was emphatic that physicians should accept the theory that **all diseases** begin when the brain is depleted or in a devitalized state. This view was encouraged in *The Secret* and by law of attraction expert Esther Hicks. Hicks described all forms of medicine, chiropractic, and even alternative treatments as "artificial aids to nature" in that they work through revitalizing the mind to heal the body, via readjustment of the cells and tissues. As it states in *The Secret*, **"Illness cannot exist in a body that has harmonious thoughts. Imperfect thoughts are the cause of all humanity's ills, including disease, poverty, and unhappiness."**

It may not come as a surprise to many who believe in vision boarding and the law of attraction that western medicine is useless. However, the implications are also that all homeopathic, naturopathic, chiropractic, herbal, Chinese, and alternative medicine treatments and therapies are also useless and unnecessary.

This mode of thinking is not new. In 1910, Wattles wrote that the right thoughts can cure all illness and disease. *"I can say of the Science of Being Well that it works, and that wherever its laws are complied with, it can no more fail to work than the science of geometry can fail to work. If the tissues of your body have not been so destroyed that continued life is impossible, you will get well, and if you will think and act in a Certain Way, you will get well."*[3] Wattles died the following year.

Similarly, Esther Hicks, performing as Abraham[4] stated, *"There is no state of physical decline or damage that you could not recover from-none-not any, if you knew it... If you wanted it and knew that you could. And that's those miracles that they talk about every day. They're not miracles at all, they are the natural order of things. But because they are rare, people think they are miraculous. They're not. That's the way it is supposed to be."*

In light of these comments it is interesting that when Esther's husband, Jerry, was diagnosed with cancer, instead of invoking higher vibrational energies and the law of attraction, he privately underwent conventional medical treatments (chemotherapy) that were ultimately unsuccessful. Esther previously claimed that Jerry was the best in the world at creating positive energies and invoking the law of attraction. Yet, ironically, when it came right down to it, he didn't believe in it or practice it.

I have challenged any believers in the law of attraction to show me how they are able to make scars disappear, cure diabetes, reverse the aging process, or regrow a limb. Thus far, no one has accepted the challenge. Why did Jerry Hicks decide to undergo conventional chemotherapy when he and Esther previously criticized this treatment? The answer is, that it was a hoax—when push comes to shove, when it involved their own personal health, they could not put their faith in the absolutely perfect law of attraction.

Let's hypothesize that the law of attraction were true. How would we explain the presence of severely disabled children? Why would babies have congenital anomalies or any diseases at all?

Esther Hicks claims that these were "old souls" arriving damaged, just for the experience. Somehow it's still their fault. I work in a children's hospital, taking care of sick children, infants, and neonates. It's hard for me to believe these young ones cause their own illnesses by virtue of their ill and dysfunctional thoughts.

I donate time and money to various charities. I travel to third world countries and take care of the poor, impoverished, and disfigured. Curiously, law of attraction experts want me to believe that these people are in that condition because they have poor thoughts. According to the law of attraction, this is the list of who we should blame:

- Victims of school shootings
- Victims of car accidents
- Victims of terrorist attacks
- Victims of the Holocaust
- Victims of the September 11 World Trade Center attacks
- Victims of rape
- Victims of tornadoes, earthquakes, hurricanes, floods, and any other natural disaster
- Anyone (including babies in neonatal intensive care units) with any disease or illness (including diabetes, heart disease, etc.)
- Anyone with cancer
- Babies with congenital heart defects
- Anyone in poverty
- Anyone with sensory impairment (visual, hearing, etc.)

It's not hard to read between the lines to see BLAME, BLAME, BLAME. Blame the Victims! The victims of rape or assault have somehow brought this negativity upon themselves. If positive *always* attracts positive, then why do good/positive people get hurt?

15

We're Not Perfect

When you read most vision board or law of attraction books, you will notice that, when its time to choose a goal, instructions will be along the lines of "Dream Big," "There are no limits," "Reasonable is not big enough," "Let your imagination run wild." Since our thoughts create our reality and our universe, there is an endless supply of anything you might want. So, get rid of your old ideas about having goals that are realistic. Consequently, vision board proponents suggest when you visualize what success looks like, you envision the *perfect* "you" or the ideal outcome. In theory, this does sound like a great idea.

Here are some quotes about *"perfect"* from vision board and law of attraction experts:

- *"The purpose of nature can be nothing else than the perfection of life. This we see from the very nature of life itself. It is the nature of life to continually advance toward more perfect living..."* (Wallace Wattles)
- *"You can think your way to the perfect state of health, the perfect body, the perfect weight, and eternal youth. You can bring it into being, through your consistent thinking of perfection."* (Rhonda Byrne)
- *"You are God in a physical body. You are perfection, You are*

the creator..." (From *The Secret*)

- "You have God potential and power to create your world..." (James Ray)
- "The pen is in your hand, and the outcome is whatever you choose." (Lisa Nichols)
- "There is no limit to what this law can do for you; dare to believe in your own ideal; think of your ideal as an already accomplished fact." (Charles Haanel)
- "The absolute truth is that the 'I' is perfect and complete; the real 'I' is spiritual and can therefore never be less than perfect; it can never have any lack, limitation, or disease." (Charles Haanel)
- "Are there any limits to this? Absolutely not. We are unlimited beings. We have no ceiling. The capabilities and the talents and the gifts and the power that is within every single individual that is on the planet, is unlimited." (Michael Bernard Beckwith)
- "If you are able to imagine it, it is not 'unrealistic.' If, from this time-space reality, you have been able to create the desire, this time-space reality has the resources to fulfill it. All that is required is your vibrational alignment with your desire." (Esther Hicks)
- "The Law of Attraction allows for infinite possibilities, infinite abundance, and infinite joy. It knows no order of difficulty, and it can change your life in every way." (Jack Canfield)

So what's wrong with wanting perfect? This sounds like a great thing to have. Well, how many of you reading this book truly have a perfect life? How many of you have made vision boards and now have a "perfect job", "perfect children", "perfect marriage", and "perfect health"? If this is the case, I find it curious that you are reading any self-help books at all. Unless you believe that things can get better than perfect.

My personal reality is I love my life. My life is great. My kids are great, my job and career are great, my relationships are great, and my health is great. Nothing is perfect and I'm great with that. Perfect is not my goal. Optimal is my goal. I don't believe in the law of attraction and so I'm very comfortable with having "optimal" as my goal, rather than "perfect".

You may ask, "Why not go for perfect since I believe in vision boards and the law of attraction?" The reason is studies have shown that fantasizing about your perfect world and your perfect life may make you feel better in the short term, but will limit your ability to transform your dreams into reality. "Perfect" fantasies are truly just wishes. Positive psychologists agree that the pursuit of perfection is associated with both unhappiness and with blaming others.[1]

On the other hand, seeking optimalism, the best, not the perfect, is associated with greater joy and happiness than seeking perfection. Moreover, unrealistic fantasies about the future, which are not based on past experiences, are associated with decreased effort, poorer performance, and less achievement. Alternatively, fantasizing with more realistic goals leads to greater effort, improved performance and a higher likelihood of success.[2]

Three important studies support the use of *realistic* over *ideal* fantasies. First, female participants in a weight loss program exposed daily to a photo of a skinny model in their weight loss diary actually *gained* weight.[3] In contrast, those who had a neutral dieting-related cue or a normal-sized model on the diary pages were more successful in losing weight. Those exposed to the ideal, thin model began to view their goals as unattainable and stepped off their dietary regimen.

The second study also involved obese women in a weight reduction program.[4] They were asked to imagine how they might behave in various food-related scenarios, such as being tempted with pizza. Those with perfect fantasies—how they would *ideally* act in a given situation (like turn down cake and ice cream) lost 26 pounds *less* than those with more realistic fantasies (I'd probably eat both my own and other people's portions).

The third study involved college students with a serious romantic interest in a classmate. They were asked to fantasize about what would happen in various scenarios like seeing their "significant other" walking into the room. Their fantasies were rated on a positive (our eyes meet and it is one of the greatest loves in history) to negative scale (not making as great a connection. I tell him I already have a boyfriend). Five months later, those with negative fantasies were more likely to have been forthcoming about their crush or taken action towards the beginning of a relationship.[2]

The philosopher Voltaire is often credited with saying, "Perfect is the enemy of good." The law of diminishing returns states that it takes about 20% effort to achieve 80% of my task and another 80% of my effort to accomplish the last 20% of the goal. My activity becomes increasingly inefficient. To achieve absolute perfection is impossible and, therefore, unrealistic (even if you believe in the law of attraction). Obviously, achieving "perfect" is less of an issue if you are relying on the universe to accomplish this for you. If you are only going to be satisfied with "perfect" health, relationships, career, and life, be prepared for lots of disappointment.

16

Placebo Effect

There are people who have reported success at realizing their dreams by creating a vision board. There are also many people who have realized their goals by throwing pennies in the wishing well, carrying a rabbit's foot, pulling apart a wishbone, wishing upon a shooting star, blowing out a candle, praying at the foot of a Hindu statue, blowing all of the seeds off a puffy dandelion, waiting until the digital clock shows 11:11 (a magical time indicating the oneness of the universe), folding one-thousand origami cranes, and wishing on bracelet charms. Some people, in fact, don't seem to have to do much and they also accomplish their goals. Does that mean these methods are ineffective? No, it means that if you are taking an active role in the process and you believe in what you are doing, it has a good possibility of working.

A placebo is a substance with no known therapeutic effects, like a sugar pill or saline solution. The placebo effect is where someone benefits in some way from receiving a non-therapeutic treatment. How could this happen? Does this mean the patient is faking a response? No, placebo does not mean that there is a hoax or fraud involved. It also does not mean the recipient is thinking themselves into a successful treatment.

The term placebo was adopted into medicine during the 18th

century and referred to decoy drugs. By the 1950s and '60s, the power of placebos was becoming well known as 30 to 60 percent of the overall therapeutic outcome was attributed to the placebo effect. Psychologist Guy Sapirstein reviewed 39 antidepressant drug studies and found the placebo was almost twice as effective as the treatment medications (50% vs. 27%).[1] A follow-up study showed an amazing 75% of depression therapy was placebo induced.

What do we know about the placebo effect? The greater your expectations and motivation that a treatment is effective, the more likely you are to have a positive response. Consistent with this thinking, the most effective placebos are injections. Next most effective are big pills and then multiple pills.[2] What else do we know? Yellow pills are great for treating depression, red pills result in greater alertness, green pills help with anxiety, and white pills are good as antacids.[3] In general, unlike with many medications, the potency of placebos often increases over time.

One famous placebo treatment was a potential anti-cancer drug named Kreboizen. In the late 1950s, Kreboizen turned out to be ineffective, but not until after it had a miraculous effect on a patient with metastatic tumors. The patient went into remission ... until he read an article showing the drug did not work as a cancer treatment.

Placebos have been shown to be wonderfully effective in the treatment of benign prostatic hypertrophy, asthma, food allergies, pain, and several other medical conditions. A biotech company came out with an anti-allergy vaccine effective in treating 75% of patients. Unfortunately (for the biotech company), 70% of patients were also successfully treated with a placebo.

One point I want to make clear, placebo does not mean faking or that it is limited to being a mind game. Studies show placebos alter levels of brain glucose metabolism, dopamine secretion, and neuronal firing, comparable to the medications they were tested against.[4,5] Placebos may trigger the release of endorphins (intrinsic pain killers) in addition to a variety of neurochemical substrates that correspond to the condition they are supposed to treat. One such class of substances released, neuropeptides, switch genes on and off as the body grows and repairs itself. This is a very powerful and very real process.

When considering the placebo effect, don't forget to take into account spontaneous successes. For example, suppose I find three hundred people who have goals of getting a new car. I divide them into three groups. I tell the first group about a great new visualization technique that is sure to get them exactly what they want. I teach them to visualize how they are going to get that new car (where they will get the money, how they will start saving, where they will start shopping, how they could trade in their old car, etc.—Action Board group). I also tell the second group about a great new visualization technique that is sure to get them exactly what they want. I teach them to visualize the exact car that they want, to the finest detail, and tell them to really picture themselves driving that new car—how it feels, how it smells, etc.—vision board group). I don't tell the third group anything.

Three months later, I check on them again to find out how successful they have been. In the Action Board group (group 1), eighty of them have gotten the cars that they wanted. In the vision board group (group 2), forty of them have accomplished their goal (according to vision board expert John Assaraf,[6] it would be one person at most—0.1% success rate—but we'll give them the benefit of the doubt). In the "do nothing" group, thirty of them have gone out and obtained the new car they wanted. So, the placebo effect (the vision board group) was actually beneficial for *ten* percent of the participants. Why ten? Because thirty percent were successful without any visualization coaching. There will always be those who achieve goals on their own accord, without any tools or strategies—spontaneously.

Let's look at the ten percent who achieved their goals through visualizing outcome. If we assume there is no law of attraction, could their visualization still be effective? Absolutely! The human brain anticipates and hopes for a good outcome. It is a self-fulfilling prophecy. The hungrier you are for achieving your goal, the more likely you are to find success with some new method. Again, this doesn't mean it's all in your head. The placebo effect is a potent stimulus for neurochemical and psychological changes where we can see, hear, taste, touch, and smell what we expect to. One thing to keep in mind is that placebos are not always beneficial. For example, it's been estimated that nineteen percent of placebo recipients manifested unexpected deteriorations in health.[1]

As discussed, a belief in the law of attraction is not simply ineffective, it is counterproductive, limiting your chance and ability to succeed. Thus, the rare successes in achieving goals with the use of vision boards may be no greater than that occurring spontaneously. Or, at the very least, the placebo effect is coming into play—brought about by individuals who are driven, motivated, and hopeful to succeed.

17

Anecdotal Evidence

Is the vision board effective? Let's look at the evidence. That's easy to do because the only evidence is anecdotal, non-scientific. The "evidence" is merely based on personal reports, hearsay, and self-interests. The self-selecting nature of positive reports (in other words, people brag when they are successful and keep quiet when they are not) combined with financial self-interests (proponents have no interest in discussing unfulfilled goals) confound our ability to see if they work.

In *The Secret,* Michael Bernard Beckwith writes, *"I've seen kidneys regenerated. I've seen cancer dissolved. I've seen eyesight improve and come back."* This is anecdotal evidence at best. I would be very surprised if this theatrical Reverend of the New Thought Movement has actually ever seen a kidney. There are many instances of cures following alternative therapies like laughter. There are also cases of spontaneous cancer remissions; this does, in fact, happen.

A perfect example of selection bias is what occurs in terms of reporting side effects from naturopathic medications. For the average person trying them out, mild side effects will not get reported anywhere. There is really no good reporting agency. Alternative medicine enthusiasts typically ignore mild side effects and ineffective therapy. Usually they take extra time to focus on any successful treatments. The little data we gather is dramatically skewed toward how great therapy is. When these same medications are studied under controlled conditions, the results are completely different. We find out the incidence of side effects is enormous. While there have been some successful treatments, the vast majority of people did not find benefit and the treatment rate is no greater than that achieved by chance alone. In other words, that particular medication had no beneficial effect; selection bias.[1]

This phenomenon appears to be active in vision boards. Those who are simply testing out vision boards will likely not report anything, while those who are predisposed to believe in the law of attraction and in the power of a vision board will be more likely to report only their successes and negate their failures. In part, this is due to a brilliant marketing scheme wherein people who are not successful blame themselves for not being focused enough or clear enough to successfully manifest their dreams. Further, if anyone who creates a vision board mentions it has not been successful, doubt and negativity are introduced, which immediately foils the chance for success. No matter how you slice it, proponents feel there is no possibility the vision board won't work or law of attraction doesn't exist. All roads must lead to proving it exists. Any evidence to the contrary is fraught with criticisms.

There are a few exceptions to this rule. Oprah's vision board coach, Martha Beck, stated, "I've made several vision boards that bombed out." If this is a universal law, why doesn't it always work? How can a knowledgeable coach not be able to use the board to fruition? As mentioned in a previous chapter, vision board expert John Assaraf also admitted to being unsuccessful at visioning being a professional basketball player.[2] Rather than admit failure, he claims that if your goal isn't achieved, but that something different but better happens, this can be counted as a successful goal completion—nice move! Even given this exemption, Assaraf still claims, **"the law of attraction does not work for 99.9% of the people that try to use it."** He is correct! Assaraf proposes many other principles and techniques that bring your conscious and subconscious mind together in harmony, replacing the importance of any law of attraction. I propose throwing away the law of attraction concept to arrive at the same conclusion.

In *The Science of Getting Rich*[3], Wallace Wattles describes multi-millionaire exceptions to the law; people who have achieved success and have not shown positivity, gratitude, etc. Examples that he cites are Rockefeller and Carnegie; explaining that their day is nearly over and a close look at their private lives reveals that they aren't really rich.

It is interesting to note that Napoleon Hill has referenced these same two individuals as achieving success through "The Secret". Hill[4] also mentions Henry Ford as being someone who has used these principles to achieve "greatness". That is curious, as he was a well-known anti-Semite who was extremely bitter toward Jews and intolerant of workers' rights. Yet, despite these glaringly negative personality traits and behaviors, he seems to have been able to invoke the law of attraction.

How does this happen? How can some people seem to invoke this law so easily and be successful, while others express one hint of doubt and their quest is over? One plausible explanation is confirmation bias—new information confirms your preconceptions and anything that contradicts your prior beliefs is avoided. Surely there will be those vision board enthusiasts who don't get this far in a book that questions the validity of something dear to them. For those individuals, the only valid evidence is that which favors the vision board and law of attraction. Anything else is blasphemy and jeopardizes their belief in the mystical powers of the universe.

Synchronicity, a phrase coined by Psychologist Carl Jung, is another phenomenon by which the law of attraction may appear to work. Synchronicity describes events that have no obvious causal connection but seem to have some meaningful relationship—some deeper, underlying conceptual framework.[5] Observers often label these events as significant coincidences. For example, you are driving down the road and see a license plate, PPY 123. The letters remind you of a puppy and this morning you were talking to your kids about maybe getting a puppy. Like the law of attraction, the underlying reason for synchronicity may be in the underlying mystery of the universe or may be due to selection bias.

We discussed the selection bias that occurs when there is self-reporting about the success of vision boards. Likewise, there is also selection bias when we focus on and remember the coincidences that work out; forgetting the enormous number of times they didn't work out. In psychology, we use the term apophenia to describe the phenomenon of believing that a pattern or meaning exists in what is actually meaningless and random data. We frequently hear, "This couldn't just be a coincidence." Well, yes, it could.

I'm thinking about a friend who I haven't seen in months and they call that same night. "Wow! This couldn't just be a coincidence." Well, out of the 70,000 fleeting thoughts that I had today, how many of them involved people I know? Probably thousands. Of the people that I thought about, how many of them didn't call me today? Thousands! I was wrong thousands of times and right once. The odds of this happening are *not* zero. Statistically, if we examine all of my daily thoughts that involve people I know, the chances are pretty good that one of them will contact me within 24 hours. Any other assumptions would be considered apophenia—seeking a pattern in random information. We have an innate propensity to look for patterns. This is not skepticism. This is realism. This does not rule out the possibility that there is magic in the universe or that God does not exist. It merely confirms that we shouldn't blindly accept theories just because they seem mystical. In terms of vision boards, as is the case in psychics, astrologers, and tarot card readers, we have to keep track of the misses, not just the hits.[6]

Unlike synchronicity, which cannot be tested experimentally, the law of attraction does lend itself to scientific investigation. I have searched the literature, in vain, for well-performed, controlled, blinded, peer-reviewed studies showing significant improvement in test scores, competitions, goal achievement, success, happiness, or subjective well-being for those creating a vision board focusing on outcomes without an associated action or completion date, or plan.

Besides confirmation bias, selection bias, apophenia, and anecdotal evidence, what else may explain the reported successes (0.1% of participants according to Assaraf) of the vision board? Perhaps this movement was started by men promoting a new concept—the importance of positive thinking. They threw in a hypothesis about the law of attraction based on erroneous and incomplete scientific knowledge, to reinforce their emphasis on the positive. The theory appealed to those looking for a mysterious means to achieve goals and eventually the law of attraction took on a life of it's own—an unintentional ruse was perpetuated.

In the book E^2, Pam Grout[7] provided several examples of "scientific experiments" demonstrating how thoughts create reality. Here is some of her "evidence": 1) Emotions affected voltage potentials within yogurt, 2) Plants and single cell organisms read your thoughts, 3) Brain waves stimulated in one person could be transferred to someone in another room. Yet, none of these "experiments" have been replicated under controlled conditions. In fact, the study designer admitted falsifying the yogurt demonstration to film a movie of the process. Grout claims nearly all food, drinks, toxins, and medicines are derived from plants that read our thoughts. Thus, she concludes our thoughts determine our physical health and weight.

Is it possible that millions of hopeful people could get caught up in such deceptions? Absolutely! Here are some other examples of great hoaxes in history:

- *Piltdown man*: In 1912, in Piltdown, England, an archaeologist named Charles Dawson found "the missing link"—a skull that was part man and part ape. The scientific community divided into skeptics and believers. Gradually, the millions of believers prevailed. In 1953, testing showed Piltdown Man to be a combination of a man's skull, orangutan's jaw, and chimp's teeth. The hoax was exposed!
- *Cardiff Giant*: A 10-foot tall "petrified man" was uncovered in 1869 by workers digging a well in Cardiff, New York. This giant gained popularity among the populace despite skepticism

by experts. It wasn't long before the hoax was discovered. George Hull created this deception and profited hugely.

- *War of the Worlds*: In 1938, Orson Welles narrated a radio broadcast depicting an alien invasion. The 'news bulletins' set off widespread panic by listeners believing that Martians had landed on Earth.
- *Cottingley Fairies*: In 1917, a series of photos depicting fairies was released. They were regarded as conclusive evidence in favor of the existence of fairies and other psychic phenomena. While public sentiment was mixed, many believed in the fairies.
- *April Fools'*: In 1983, History Professor Joseph Boskin was interviewed about the origins of April Fools' Day. He made up a story about jesters petitioning the emperor of Rome to allow one of the Jjsters, Kugel, the chance to rule Rome for one day, April 1—a day of silliness. This fictitious story spread across the country like wildfire, even after the author admitted the fraud.
- *Naked Stranger:* In 1969, a bored housewife, Penelope Ashe, wrote a trashy novel called *Naked Came the Stranger*. Ashe went on tour and the book became widely read. It turns out the real author was columnist Mike McGrady who wrote the worst book that he could muster, to expose booksellers for selling poorly written books. He got his sister-in-law, Ashe, to play the role of the author. The book quickly sold 20,000 copies and even after the hoax was revealed continued to sell well—spending 15 weeks on the *Times*'s bestseller list. To date, more than 400,000 copies have been sold.
- *Bathtubs:* In 1917, humorist HL Mencken wrote an essay called "*A Neglected Anniversary.*" He described how the bathtub only

caught on after Millard Fillmore installed one in the White House on Dec. 20th and lamented about the anniversary being forgotten. He admitted the whole tale was made up, but the story's popularity snowballed. It became highly referenced and even cited on the floor of Congress. To this day, it is still a widely believed legend.

- *Loch Ness Monster:* In 1934, gynecologist Robert Wilson snapped a photo of a giant prehistoric monster in Loch Ness, Scotland. The creature gained worldwide attention, sparking hundreds of investigations into finding out more information about the beast. It wasn't until 60 years later that Christian Spurling admitted to the hoax. He described how his father-in-law had created the picture with a fake monster head placed on a toy submarine. Dr. Wilson submitted the photo to give it credibility. Yet millions still believe. *Nine years after the hoax was revealed,* the BBC used 600 separate sonar beams and satellite navigation and proved no such beast exists. Despite this data and the admission of fraud, the Loch Ness Monster industry is thriving, bringing about $2 million to the area each year.

In summary, the fact that there are millions who believe in a law of attraction is not, in and of itself, evidence such a law exists. Disciples bring many forms of bias to the table and start the discussion with a predilection to believe in something mystic. We see things that we want to see and hear things that we want to hear. We especially look for any data or evidence that will support our preconceived biases and disregard or are critical regarding evidence against. There are many subjective things in our universe that need not be subject to scientific scrutiny such as philosophy, religion, and beauty. In contrast, scientific theories such as gravity and the law of attraction should stand up against scientific scrutiny. If there is no conceivable way to disprove a scientific theory, then that theory is worth nothing in terms of its ability to predict your future. Pam Grout[7] propounds that, to be valid scientifically, a theory should be falsifiable. However, she also claims the law of attraction is perfect. So, if it doesn't work, Grout argues, it's your fault. In other words, there is no way to disprove the theory.

My comments about the law of attraction are specific to this theory. My thoughts are not generalizable to beliefs in God or energy in the universe or any other "universal" law. I am a believer in mysticism, but I do not believe in every mystical hypothesis proposed. When a theory limits our ability to achieve goals and is based on faulty science, I look for better theories. Being open to the possibility there is no law of attraction will be your invitation to a newfound empowerment. It will help you move beyond the 0.1% of the population who can achieve their dreams *via* the law of attraction.

18

Throw Away Your Vision Board

You may be new to the world of vision boards and open-minded about the usefulness of the vision board as a goal setting tool, or you may be a vision board devotee and view the previous discussion as blasphemy. I realize when I discuss vision boards and the law of attraction, there is a wide range of opinions that vary from "Of course there's no law of attraction," to "How can you fathom a world without the law of attraction?" I would like to begin by providing a brief summary of some of the arguments against the existence of the law of attraction. Then I will reveal why vision boards, based on the law of attraction, are doomed to fail from the outset.

Law of Attraction

To begin, the law of attraction was founded in the late 1800s and really has a foundational basis in erroneous pseudoscience—ether in the brain, high frequency thought energy, thought-specific vibrations, the more intensely you think about something the higher it's thought potency, thought can only travel through ether, magnetism means like attracts like, etc. It is enticing for some to believe the founders of this school of thought had some theories that turned out to be supported by metaphysics and quantum mechanics. Unfortunately, this is not the case. It is true that particle physics has shown we are all made of the same stuff. That is, the brain has electrical activity, and subatomic particles vibrate. Yet, there are many essential components of the law of attraction theory that have been disproven or are not supported by any evidence. It makes this scientific theory unfounded and baseless. For some of you, that knowledge may be enough to cause you to turn back, give up your beliefs, and begin your search for a better, evidence-based system to achieve your goals. If I'm describing you, you may choose to skip the following discussion and fast-forward to the "Action Board" section of this book where you will learn to apply a systematic, proven system to accomplish what you've been waiting so long to do.

For others, having the law of attraction labeled as metaphysical *pseudo*science does not matter. You may view the law of attraction as a belief system, similar to having a belief in God or a universal energy system. For you it may be a form of religion and, as such, does not require a base in scientific reality. "You can't prove God and I'm okay with that." You are also the ones likely to take this as a personal assault and be insulted by any attempts to expose and de-mystify this 'law'. You may turn this back, opining that this book is too scientific or close-minded. You may just ignore any evidence to the contrary; practicing apophenia—"My mind is made up, don't confuse me with the facts!"

When it comes to discussing mysticism and universal laws, the word "evidence" has taken on a negative connotation. It leads to a defensive posture wherein believers default to "You are too entrenched in western medicine and science to appreciate that the universe may have mystical energies." If you find it in your hearts to read on, please understand that this is not an attempt to eliminate mysticism from the universe. This is merely a logical and realistic treatise showing that this particular type of mystical belief is not science, is not real, and is not healthy.

This next section is addressed to the readers who have been inculcated into the law of attraction world. Please note I do indeed believe in God and in a life-sustaining energy source. I believe in Kabbalah—Jewish mysticism—and I believe that sometimes God or the universe may have other plans for us that we don't always understand. There is no proof for my beliefs. They are unsubstantiated and that's why they are 'beliefs'. Just as importantly, you can't disprove a belief in God. Having a belief in God or in a universal, life-sustaining energy does not in and of itself necessarily predict anything that is testable. For example, if God exists, there are still many plausible explanations for why there are bad people in the world or why bad things happen to good people. It is impossible, despite atheist arguments, to disprove an existence or lack of existence of God or universal energy. These beliefs make no predictions that lend themselves to be tested, since they vary depending on responses from God or the universe. We can't pretend to predict how God or the universe might respond to our thoughts or actions.

How do these beliefs differ from a belief in the law of attraction? The concept of a universal law of attraction implicitly carries with it certain definitive predictions, which can be empirically tested. When we look closely at these predictions, they do not hold up to scrutiny. The law of attraction is unable to explain why babies have diseases, why Tibetan monks get ill, why negative people can become successful, and why it's so difficult to achieve goals using such a powerful, universal tool. The fact that most people using the law of attraction are unsuccessful is like saying that the law of gravity sometimes works and sometimes doesn't. The law of gravity makes certain predictions that are easy to test.

Moreover, law of attraction proponents point out that this law is universal, perfect, and always works whether you understand it or not. If this is the case, why do so many experts have to teach us how to use it? Why do they keep selling us more and more information on "secrets" about the law? I've never had to buy a book or course or be coached on how to use gravity. It seems to work continuously, all the time, every place I've been, whether I think about it or not. THAT is a universal law.

Let's summarize some of the predictions of this "universal and perfect" law of attraction. Every specific thought you have (approximately 70,000 per day) has a specific frequency or wavelength of energy that leaves your brain, travels around the world through the ether and creates whatever you were thinking about in some kind of "Formless stuff". As with magnets, like ALWAYS attracts like. Further, EVERY bad thing that you or anyone else has ever experienced is their fault. There are no accidents. Even God would not be able to change these plans. You brought it on yourself. If you have had a bad relationship or any kind of illness or disease, you are to blame.

Let's look at a few hypothetical situations. You are in a properly parked car and a drunk driver hits you from behind. You hit your head on the windshield and you are bleeding. Your child is sitting in the backseat and breaks her arm. When the police arrive, they ask you what happened and, as a believer in the law of attraction, you say, "It's all my fault, officer. I caused this accident" (or did your daughter cause it?). If you think about saying anything else, it would be a lie and you would get caught up in a negative spiral of deceit and negativity, never accomplishing any of your goals. Similarly, if you are getting a divorce and believe in the law of attraction, I hope you admit to the judge the reason your marriage failed was entirely your fault. Your aging mother gets sick because her caretaker gave her spoiled food and then didn't call the doctor. That's all your mother's fault because she brought this on herself (including the aging part). Remember, if you believe in the law of attraction, there is no aging, there is no disease other than that which you bring on yourself, and there are no accidents. These are not silly examples. These are real life examples if you want to live a life sincere with your beliefs in this law.

The law of attraction concept is inherently chock-full of blame; blaming yourself when you don't achieve your goals, blaming others for their lots in life. The law of attraction predicts that thinking about or associating in any way with people who are mentally, physically, emotionally, spiritually, or psychologically not perfect will ALWAYS introduce those negatives into your life. Whether you are trying to help others or joining a support group, it is not healthy for you. According to the law of attraction, all illnesses and diseases occur due to dysfunctional thoughts—avoid these people. For example: steer clear of all of the babies in the neonatal and pediatric intensive care units; the school children who get shot by mentally ill terrorists; the impoverished millions around the world hoping to find a scrap of food; patients with breast cancer, etc. The law of attraction is not a friendly law. It is an anti-empathy and anti-compassion law.

If I were to sincerely believe in the law of attraction, I would not be able to attend any support groups, donate my time to medical missions, give to any charity, or be a coach, personal trainer, or physician. The good news is I would have a lot of extra time to sit and visualize, as I'd be out of a job!

If I truly believed in the law of attraction, I would not be able to find out about the world around me. As Rhonda Byrne has stated, "When I discovered The Secret I made a decision that I would not watch the news or read newspapers anymore..." I don't fault her for this line of thinking. She is right. If you believe that this is a universal and perfect law and you want to benefit from it, that is what you too should do. No newspapers, no charities, no negativity.

If I truly believed in the law of attraction, I would visualize the perfect world, perfect health, perfect friends, perfect marriage, perfect job and career. Anything other than that would bring me negativity and destroy my chances of having those things. The consequence of this mode of thinking is I should make no plans, prepare for no obstacles, and take no actions. This is not true and unrealistic. Yes, in fact, you can take 'inspired action', but realize that, according to law of attraction experts, the universe appears to be more sensitive to negative cues than positive ones. We are told that even apparently inconsequential habits like parking your car in the middle of the garage would obliterate your chances of ever discovering your soul mate (they'd have no place to park).

It is hard to go out into the world and be shielded from any negative actions, thoughts, sights, or sounds. Removing yourself from reality to spend the day visualizing is not being mindful in the present. Yet, when you stop visualizing and come back to reality, you are no longer able to completely fulfill the requirements for the law of attraction—a double-edged sword!

Vision Boards

I've been spending a lot of time on the law of attraction. How does this relate to vision boards? As I stated at the beginning of this book, not all vision boards are created equal. There are some types of vision boards that take an in-depth look at how and why you are setting your goals and have incorporated scientific theory behind goal achievement. These are systems based on sound reasoning and realistic principles, not simply cutting out pictures and wishing upon a board. Two such systems are those sold by John Assaraf and Jack Canfield. These are both highly successful individuals whose 'systems' are based on sound foundations. Both contributed to the book *The Secret* and now that they are on their own, tell a much different story about how to actually achieve goals. For them, the law of attraction now plays a much smaller role, acting in the background as a 'support structure'. However, as good as their systems appear, Assaraf's and Canfield's systems are still limited in their potential due to their reliance on the law of attraction.

If these systems are limited in their effectiveness, why are people still appearing to benefit? The answer is simple and twofold. First, their clients only have a superficial understanding of the law of attraction. The law is discussed in terms that are useful for their programs, but offer no details about their true implications. Their clients don't fully appreciate what they are buying into and the systems are not based on any law of attraction. This leads to the second part of the answer. They both teach systems that in many ways contradict what you should be doing if you believe in the law of attraction. They both give to charities. They both help people less fortunate than themselves. They both believe in planning and helping other people plan. They both believe in value-based goals. They both believe in the importance of looking at what you don't want. They both believe in the power of failure and challenge. They both believe in the necessity of taking action. In summary, they both ignore and act contradictory to the law of attraction.

Many vision board experts maintain their faith in the law of attraction, even while admitting that the chance of success by invoking this law is exceedingly rare, 0.1%.[1] This is not because it is complicated. It is because such a law doesn't exist. Because of the lack of success using this law, there are now multitudes of books that provide clues, cues, keys, and secrets about how to properly invoke this law.[1-11]

Originally, to activate the law of attraction, you simply needed to think about what you wanted (thoughts create the world). Then it became about what you thought *and* what you said (Don't say, "lose weight" or you'll get "weight"). That soon became what you thought, said, and felt (emotions became more important). Now even that is not enough. It turns out that we need to help the universe, make plans, boost our energy levels, overcome emotional blocks, and take action.

The modern day concept of vision boards was popularized as a mechanism by which we could utilize and enforce the law of attraction. Thus, the law of attraction unfortunately happens to be a core feature and backbone of vision board methodologies. When you are creating a vision board and envisioning a perfect future with your perfect spouse, living in your perfect house, going to your perfect job and going on the perfect vacation with your perfect kids, good luck! You are living a mindless and unrealistic existence that will be fraught with disappointment and dissatisfaction. This type of visualization has been shown to be inferior to process or task methods. Yet, task visualization is inconsistent with the law of attraction because it incorporates obstacles, planning, and action steps. My comments are not meant to insult vision board proponents. They are merely meant to give you a realistic appraisal of why you have been unsuccessful at achieving most of your goals by relying on the law of attraction.

You are not alone. Many people are coming to the same conclusions; the law of attraction does not work as advertised. The founders supposed it to be so, but that doesn't make it real. Once you truly understand the law of attraction and the logic behind these fallacies and false claims, it is apparent that the inductive reasoning of "It doesn't matter if you believe in it because it is. We don't have to prove it, because it is. We can't demonstrate it, but it is," does not hold up. It is a philosophy of disempowerment.

Here's a conversation between my vision board coach (VBC) and me.

VBC: "Following the law of attraction is incredibly easy and everyone can do it."

Farber: "Is that true?"

VBC: "Oh yes. In fact, you are doing it right now, whether you know it or not."

Farber: "What does it involve?"

VBC: "Positive ALWAYS attracts positive. Think positive thoughts and you'll send positive vibrations into the universe and the universe will create anything that you want. Think big and abundantly. Make it very specific. Visualize it. Nothing is too big!"

Farber: "Okay, then I'll guess I'll do it. I'm visualizing a red brick house with an awning and 40 by 60 foot swimming pool in the back, 5 bedrooms, 3 baths, and circular staircase. The house is #5820 Lake Drive in River Hills. When I open the door for the first time, there are a million dollar bills lying in the middle of the grand foyer."

VBC: "Wow, some visualization. Have you been to the house at that address before?"

Farber: "I've been to that address. But the house at that address is a small, one-story ranch with no yard. I'm visualizing that I just won the house in a lottery. It's really an amazing feeling to have this house. I've dreamt about it literally for years and now to think that I really own it…"

VBC: "Wait a minute. Not so fast. There's more to the story. You need to connect your conscious to your subconscious, make sure that the stars are in line, the ether jar is full, and that you have completely visualized what it looks and feels like."

Farber: "I'm doing that now. I own this thing. Congratulate me. I'm driving over there now to get the money from the grand foyer…"

VBC: "It's not going to be there yet. You can't put a time limit on the universe. The universe is setting things up in motion to remove the house that is there and start the seeds of your house in that spot."

Farber: "You're teasing me to see if I'll break and be negative. It won't work. I know that house is there now because I've visualized it with my heart and soul, conscious and subconscious. It is mine and I'm going to see it now."

VBC: "I don't recommend that. It's probably not going to be there."

The vision board coach was right. It wasn't there. How did they know? Because you can't just submit a vision and choose from the law of the universe catalog for material abundance.

It is vital that you realize these are not my interpretations of this law and these are not 'radical' explanations. These are written facts and descriptions from the founders and experts of the law of attraction. When I discuss these predictions with law of attraction proponents, they often say that they "believe in the law in general, but not in all of that other stuff." Well, that "other stuff" is part of the law. You can't have just part of a universal law. When the law is LIKE *ALWAYS* ATTRACTS LIKE, which of the four words would you throw out? If you want to throw out the word "ALWAYS", then it is no longer a universal law and then you need to read the next chapter to find out what it becomes…

On the surface, the law of attraction sounds very appealing. It appeals to our sense of responsibility and power to control our future. It sounds so empowering and mystical. We usually associate "mystical" with openness, compassion, and spirituality. Who wouldn't like some of that? But that's not what this law of attraction offers us. It is disturbing that, in the face of mounting countervailing reality, an enormous failure rate, an inability to make any accurate predictions, and a preponderance of opposing evidence, there are still so many in support of a law of attraction theory.

I do not have a bias against vision boards. I have a bias towards utilizing health, wellness, goal setting, and positivity techniques that work.

In the next section you'll be introduced to a newer tool, the **Action Board**. The Action Board addresses the deficiencies in vision boards and replaces the law of attraction with something much better. In contrast to vision boards, Action Boards help you ACHIEVE rather than just set goals.

Section II

Action Boards

19

Introduction to Action Boards

The previous section analyzed the negative issues involved in vision boards. The most profound of which revolved around the law of attraction. In the end, the message is to THROW AWAY YOUR VISION BOARD! This should come as no surprise and with no regret if you've been using one. It has probably been ineffective, left you feeling unfulfilled and your goals unrealized. Remember, even John Assaraf, well-known vision board and law of attraction expert, has stated that there is a *99.9% failure rate*[1] for those using vision boards. You're probably ready to throw the thing away.

Where does that leave you? I've been hinting at something better, a more effective way to achieve that transcends pop-psychology and metaphysical pseudoscience. What I'm referring to is the ACTION BOARD.

"What is an Action Board?"

Action Boards are vision boards on steroids. They are evidence-based goal achievement tools. In other words, Action Boards don't just use techniques that 'feel good'. They are based on ground-breaking mind-brain research, incorporating methods that have been conclusively shown to be effective for *all* of your goals, not just material abundance.

Are you doing what you truly want to do? Are you living the life of your dreams? Are you stuck in a dead-end job? Are you in an unfulfilling relationship? Are you unhappy with your health, wealth, or body image? Are you frustrated with the lack of success that you've had with your vision board or other self-help methods that didn't work?

Well, get ready for a truly amazing life! You are about to learn the key to achieve your dreams, wishes, hopes, and goals. The secret about this system is that *you* play an active role. As with vision boards, you can start the process by sitting on the couch and visualizing. But that's where the similarity ends. You'll play an active role in crafting your inspired action plan to a life of confidence, well-being, and success.

Some of you may be worried that when you throw away your vision board, you will also be throwing away some of the principles and concepts that initially turned you on to the vision board. You may be apprehensive about getting rid of certain ways of looking at the world that innately appealed to your sense of how you hope the universe works. This is not the case. Eliminating the law of attraction does not remove those concepts you love about vision boards; it actually makes those concepts more important and effective.

"What do Action Boards not eliminate?"

Positive thinking: Action Boards do not eliminate or in any way decrease your belief in the power of positive thinking. They are strongly based in positive psychology. As a card-carrying member of the International Positive Psychology Association and writer for the "happiness" section of *Psychology Today*, I believe in optimism. I also believe in hope and gratitude. In contrast to vision boards, perfection (which is not a tenet of positive psychology) is not a healthy pursuit. It is not enough to study positive psychology. We should believe in it and live it. Many vision board devotees, blinded by their love for the law of attraction, feel eliminating this law eliminates some of the focus on positivity. This is not so. The Action Board is based on a positivity psychology outlook.

Visualization: Action Boards strongly enforce the use of visualization techniques. They are potent tools that, if used correctly, can help you achieve success and greatness. The Action Board introduces DIVINE visualization that incorporates both outcome and task/process visualization techniques to make it much more effective and engaging.

Mysticism: The Action Board eliminates the law of attraction, not mysticism. I believe in mystical Kabbalah and in other aspects of mysticism. There are many things that cannot yet be explained and that we may never explain. Believing in these things can be energizing and fulfilling. However, in the case of the law of attraction, belief can be hazardous and unhealthy.

Spirituality: The Action Board does not preclude the incorporation of spirituality. We are spiritual beings. What you put out into the universe you are more likely to get back. This may be a result of universal energy, this may be due to God's influence, or this may be a direct result of social, cognitive, and positive psychology. You may view spirituality as a strength you will use to achieve goals or a value upon which to base your goals.

Accountability: The Action Board enforces personal accountability, yet reduces the negativity of self-blame inherent in every law of the attraction-based vision board. We have complete control over the internal events in our lives (what you think about and the feelings that are associated with those thoughts), and more limited control over external events. Accidents, illnesses, diseases, natural disasters, and terrorist attacks are not necessarily linked to your thoughts.

Planning and Action: Vision boards focus on cutting out pictures and directing your intention to the universe manifesting the outcome. You are the middleman in this process. Action Boards help you strategically plan and prepare to take *Inspired Action* based on your value-based goals. Not all action is created equal. You will see how using the Key to Achieve Principles allows you to quickly develop inspired action and enjoy the journey.

These statements reveal some of the things that clients have told me they initially loved about the idea of a vision board.
- "You get back what you put in."
- "We are magnets, attracting what we are most passionate about."
- "Positive brings about positive."
- "The universe is full of energy."
- "Thoughts are important in shaping your behavior and destiny."
- "We are energy."
- "We are responsible for our future."
- "Visualize your future to make it come true."
- "The focus on positivity."
- "The concept of inspired action."

If you were attracted to vision boards because of the above quotes, do not fret. You will still be able to apply all of these concepts when using the Action Board.

"How do Action Boards differ from vision boards?"

The most important difference between Action Boards and vision boards is the elimination of the *law* of attraction, its replacement being the *principle* of attraction. This seemingly minor change moves the Action Board out of the 19th century and into the 21st century. This simple but critical upgrade allows us to:

- Base goal setting on the eight ***Key-to-Achieve*** principles
- More appropriately be ***accountable***
- ***Eliminate self-blame***
- ***Reduce blaming others*** for their suffering
- Focus on ***value-based goals***
- Pursue goals ***mindfully*** in the present
- Establish our ***dominoes*** - our personal journey
- Fully utilize the power of ***positive psychology***
- Show ***gratitude*** for the process
- Introduce the concept of ***DIVINE visualization***
- ***Plan*** positively
- Incorporate ***inspired action*** steps
- Appreciate and ***prepare*** for future challenges
- Replace failures with ***successes***
- ***Celebrate*** our victories

The following chapters will describe in more detail the Key to Achieve Principles (Chapter 20) behind the Action Board and the Components (Chapter 21) that comprise the Action Board—it's more than pretty pictures! Positive thoughts without positive actions are positively a waste of time! Let's take some Inspired Action and read on!

20

Principles: The Key to Achieve

Can you get what you want from life by asking the universe, believing in ether and mind control, and then waiting for a special UPS delivery package containing your Maserati? The answer is, unequivocally, no! With little effort comes little respect and appreciation for the outcome. There is no opportunity to develop resilience or the ability to rise to a challenge, and no life experience. The real 'secret' lies in the principles of "Key to Achieve."

You have the ability to get everything that you want from life. The secret lies in integrating several key principles and using them in harmony with each other. Here are a few more secrets: 1) These key principles apply to any and all of your goals, 2) You already possess "The Key to Achieve", 3) It is likely that any goals you have already accomplished in your life were achieved by using these key principles—even if you didn't realize you were doing it.

This chapter will describe each of the Eight Key-to-Achieve Principles that have been incorporated into the Action Board.

1. ***Accountability***:

Life does not happen to you—you happen to life. Making things happen is your responsibility. Acknowledging your ability to choose is empowering.[1] It is the first step on your journey to grow and learn, develop and experience. Relinquishing control of your decisions to anyone else or even to the 'Universe' provides us with the freedom to blame someone else if we do not succeed.

This doesn't mean you are in control of all facets of your life. You do not control what other people do, think, feel, or how they act. You do not control the weather and cannot stop tornadoes from occurring by wishing them away. If we believe that the attainment of your goals is only dependent on how well you visualize that they've already happened, then you are more likely to blame yourself for every failure. Action Boards are about empowerment, not about blaming—yourself or others. This is a principle that one of my mentor's, success guru, Dr. Stephen Covey, included in the *7 Habits of Highly Effective People*.[2]

2. *Values*:

Establishing goals based on your core values infuses them with deeper meaning and energizes you to pursue them passionately. The brevity of this section does not reflect its importance. Living a life based on your values was the foundation for Dr. Stephen Covey's analysis of achieving a balanced and satisfying life.[3]

With the Action Board, you set your goals based on your deep-seated desires, not fleeting wants. Identifying your values elevates their degree of importance in your life. When your values and goals are in alignment, you create a powerful and positive cycle of energy, success, and satisfaction; a purpose-driven life.

3. *Mindfulness*:

Being mindful is being involved and aware in a moment-to-moment way. Eckhart Tolle called it the *Power of Now*.[4] Mindfulness brings about great health and wellness benefits; greater life satisfaction. The law of attraction has us focus on outcome and the future. One of the Keys to Achieve is using a mindful approach—appreciating the process, the journey and where we are right now at this moment. Getting dropped off on the top of Mount Everest will not bring you the same satisfaction and fulfillment that would be achieved through a successful climb.

Living as if a possible future has already happened means that you are not living presently, whereas being fully engaged in and appreciating the process enhances mindfulness. Multiple studies show how much more beneficial it is to visualize a process (motivating) than simply visualizing the outcome (demotivating).[5]

Research has shown that the benefits of mindfulness are not just in your mind; they are also in your brain. Mindfulness increases the thickness of brain areas involved in sensation and decision-making. Focusing on mindfulness makes you less sensitive to pain and better able to make important decisions. These are great characteristics for people driven to achieve their goals. Furthermore, mindfulness also changes the electrical connections in the brain that inhibit internal 'chatter' and strengthen specific brain circuits,[6] allowing you to focus your attention on what you want most to accomplish. This is a formula for success. Added benefits? Mindfulness is an effective treatment for many psychological ills and even treating chronic pain!

4. *Positivity*:

The Action Board incorporates a variety of beneficial positive psychology topics[7-10] such as: **Strengths** – your personal talents and abilities, **Flow** – an exhilarating feeling of being in the zone, **Positive communication** – using positive verbiage with positive emotions benefits relationships, another essential ingredient in achieving success, **Hope and Optimism** – the belief that good things will happen in the future and that you have the power and ability to help make that happen, **Resilience** – the fortitude to pursue your goals despite significant obstacles, **Gratitude** – being thankful for what you have, the gifts that you are given, and the process by which you can achieve all that you need, **Celebrations** – observing small accomplishments along the way, **Meaning** – finding deeper meaning for your beliefs and actions; an inspirational belief in something greater than yourself, **Making Lemonade**[11] – cognitive restructuring; converting apparently 'bad' things into 'good' things to dispute our negative thoughts and derive beneficial emotional consequences.

Bringing positive psychology into goal setting motivates you, inspires you, and guarantees happiness along the way. The principle of positivity is not simply having a positive mental attitude; it is living a life of positivity.

5. *Attraction*:

I have been certified as an Advanced Practitioner of the Law of Attraction from one of the foremost authorities in the world (Dr. Joe Vitale). I have done extensive research on the topic and read almost every book written on the subject. I can now, with certainty, state that the ***law*** of attraction does not exist!

There is, however, a ***principle*** of attraction.[12] What's the difference between the law of attraction and principle of attraction? *Law*: Like *Always* Attracts Like, *Principle*: Like *Tends* to Attract Like.

Many people, after understanding the negative consequences of the law of attraction (such as blaming rape victims, child abuse victims, and ill babies for their problems), say, "I still believe in it, but take out the word *always*." When you take out the word "always", it is no longer a universal law. It is a *principle*.

Positive people tend to attract other positive people, tend to get better jobs, tend to have more successful careers, tend to be more altruistic, often have better relationships, improved health, and often live longer. Positive people have personality traits that help them achieve goals. This is not magic and is not a universal law. It is a well-researched, social scientific phenomenon.

Let's look at some predictions. The principle of attraction predicts that if you are positive and optimistic, you will tend to live longer and be healthier. This has been verified in research studies. Studies have shown that optimistic people live on average four to ten years longer than pessimistic people. One study looked at thousands of elderly people and showed that the most optimistic people were 45% less likely to die from all causes, at any given age. Realize that because it is true for the average person, this does not make it true for every individual, as the law of attraction would predict.

The principle of attraction correctly predicts the average optimistic person has an enhanced immune system and is healthier than the average pessimistic person. Yet, there will be individuals within the positive/optimistic group who are not healthy and have a weaker immune system (in contrast to the *law* of attraction). Those who have a blind love for the law of attraction will likely not be swayed by this data. They may argue that anyone who had an illness was secretly negative and pessimistic. Thus, the law of attraction could explain everything (in retrospect) but not predict anything prospectively. If you cannot use a theory to predict anything and you cannot disprove it, then it is not a good scientific theory.

While the law of attraction involves a lot of blaming—both self and others—a principle of attraction eliminates blaming. You do not control the universe. The soldier isn't to blame for not regenerating his amputated legs, despite his best efforts using the law of attraction. You are not to blame for someone hitting your car while you were properly parked. The kids at Newtown, Connecticut weren't to blame for the terrorist shooting they experienced. The babies that I take care of in the Neonatal Intensive Care Unit are not to blame for their illnesses. Thus, with the law of attraction, you get blaming. With the principle of attraction, you get empathy.

The *law* of attraction states you can cure and avoid all illness, disease, and accidents, reverse aging, and even make scars disappear by positive thoughts. The *principle* of attraction explains that positive thoughts and actions will certainly aid in the recovery of and help prevent many illnesses and diseases; but won't prevent death or eliminate scarring.

Further, the law of attraction contends *all* victims of rape, child abuse, spousal abuse, diseases, childhood illnesses, accidents, natural disasters, Third World poverty, holocaust, slavery, cancer, etc. are to blame for their lot in life. On the other hand, the principle of attraction asserts we should have empathy for these victims. A small percentage of them may have had some negative role in their experience, however the vast majority of them could have been victims despite having beautiful, loving, happy, optimistic thoughts.

Whatever you put out into the universe, you will tend to get back more of the same. Positive emotions, feelings, words, and actions usually lead to more positive things happening. If you are a positive person, positive people will often surround you. It just makes sense on all levels.

6. ***Dominoes*:**

Each goal is established with mini-goals and challenges along the way. With a vision board you avoid thinking about challenges. Just thinking about them would bring about negative consequences. In the Action Board, challenges can be hugely inspiring; providing a chance for us to learn, grow, and become even more empowered.

In addition, the Action Board utilizes the domino theory, with dominoes representing each step along the path, leading to the final goal. Obstacles, challenges, and events along the way become goals that we want to conquer—dominoes to knock down.[13,1]

We have the power to choose where we place our dominoes and appreciate our personal role in making our hopes, goals, and dreams come true. Every domino we knock down is an accomplishment to celebrate, an empowering journey improving our self-worth and self-esteem. This is a positive, mindful development where you take responsibility, enjoy the process, and celebrate your multiple victories. What could be better than that?

7. ***Divine Visualization*:**

There are plenty of well-performed, randomized studies investigating the most effective visualization techniques.[15-20] The Action Board incorporates these scientific results into a Key Principle called ***DIVINE*** Visualization:

- ***Define*** a value-based goal that aligns with your principles.
- ***Inquire*** about what you optimistically want to achieve.
- ***Visualize*** the outcome. How will it look and feel?
- ***Identify*** where you are now, your strengths, motivation, and situation.
- ***Need*** assessment for what it will take to go from where you are to

where you want to be.
- *Envision* the process. Visualize yourself doing what it takes to achieve your goal.

Visualization is important to achieving goals. Yet, not all visualization is created equal. Effective visualization is more than just having a pictorial representation of the perfect future. DIVINE visualization focuses on *three* components supercharging it to help you achieve.

First, DIVINE visualization links the present directly to the future. This connection sends a powerful signal to your conscious and subconscious minds. The conscious and subconscious minds process information very differently and each is critical to help you achieve goals. The conscious mind is slower and less efficient, it is *the* source of logical planning, reason, and analysis. The subconscious mind is brilliant at rapidly processing billions of bits of information and keeping you focused. To the subconscious mind, your visualizations are real. The process of DIVINE visualization directs the transfer of information from your conscious—goal *setting*—mind to your subconscious – goal *getting*—mind.

Second, the most effective visualizations are *process* or task visualizations where you envision 'doing', not 'having' (See Chapters 12 and 15). *Outcome* visualizations (law of attraction) are limited in their success. There are several benefits to *process* visualization: more profound brain activation, greater physiological and psychological motivation, and enhanced novel neural pathways—neuroplasticity. Scientists have shown that simply visualizing the exercises improves muscle strength almost as much as actually doing them. It turns out that process visualization activates the same brain areas as when you physically move the muscles. Visualizing the journey leads to greater motivation and greater success in all areas of life. These are not opinions; they are research-based findings on the most effective mental simulation techniques.

Third, the DIVINE visualization system reprograms the reticular activating system (RAS). Unlike most 'experts' on the law of attraction who discuss the RAS, I have actually measured brain activity in the RAS in a laboratory. The RAS is a network of long nerve pathways in your brainstem. In addition to controlling a lot of bodily functions, the RAS is the attention-focus center. It takes all of the billions of bits of sensory information, filters them, and relays them to higher brain centers (such as the prefrontal cortex) for processing.

Here's an example of how it works (complete each number before moving on. Don't cheat by looking ahead).

1) Think about the color *blue*. Look around your room for 10 seconds and count all of the *blue* objects.

2) Did you take a good look around for *blue* objects? Excellent.

3) Now answer this question, how many *red* objects are there?

If you are like most people, you will have no idea how many red objects are around you even though you just looked at each of them. This is the RAS in action! It sifts through loads of information to focus on what you're looking for. That's what makes the RAS so important in goal achieving. This is also one of the brain centers that is responsible for the erroneous notion of the law of attraction since the RAS will help us find more of whatever we are focusing on—what we think is what we get! The process of DIVINE visualization trains the RAS to make it more goal-directed and more effective. Visualization should be **PRO** = **P**rocess-Driven, **R**ealistic, and **O**ptimistic. The DIVINE visualization process capitalizes on these new research findings to bring you the most motivating and effective system possible.

8. Inspired Action

Action separates dreaming from doing. As discussed previously, some vision board proponents recommend taking only "inspired action." However, taking any action suggests that you have doubt as to the ability of the universe to bring you what you want. Doubt is negativity. Besides, how can you be justified in taking action if you are supposed to believe and act as if you have already attained the object of your desire?

A principle, rather than a law, of attraction settles this issue. A principle of attraction does not guarantee delivery. Rather, it requires you to take an active role in your destiny. With a belief in economy of motion, taking some action is not necessarily better than taking no action. However, action arising out of principles, which are energized by visualizations, will be deep-seated and meaningful. It will be a driving force and inspiration in your life. As success coach Zig Zigler has claimed, "Do it, and then you will feel motivated to do it." This value-based, energized action, which necessarily arises from creating an Action Board, will always be INSPIRED.

21

Components

Whether it's a dream board, treasure map, or vision board, millions of people create physical representations of their deepest desires. These displays focus their attention, delineate their dreams in a visual sense, and help manifest their goals by invoking the law of attraction.

What is the difference between a vision board and Action Board?

In general, most vision boards are comprised of pictures, photos, and/or motivational slogans. Even when the vision board system is more involved and is based on deeper concepts, the vision board rarely incorporates these other factors into the board. Questions regarding the vision board typically revolve around whether to group pictures, whether to have some sort of focus in the center of the board, and whether to include a photo of you in the center. There are no right or wrong ways to construct a vision board. In contrast, the Action Board consists of ten components. Each serve unique functions to help motivate, visualize, take inspired action steps, achieve goals, and celebrate successes.

Realize that having a basic understanding of the Key to Achieve Principles (Chapter 20) will help direct and guide you while you create a board. Identifying your goals within the context of your values and principles is crucial to setting up attainable and satisfying goals.

In brief, here are the ten essential components to the Action Board that utilize the eight Key to Achieve Principles:

1) *Dominator statement*

The dominator statement acts like your personal motivating vision statement. It conveys a general sense of what is important and your intentions. The dominator statement helps guide your goal-directed behavior. Goals based only on wants are like New Year's Resolutions—destined to fail. What's missing? Your deepest, sincerest personal values that inspire you to choose this goal in the first place. Consider one of these value areas to begin your journey:

- Family and Home
- Spiritual and Ethical
- Financial and Career
- Physical and Health
- Social and Cultural
- Mental and Educational
- Leisure
- Adventure

Here are a few examples of some dominator statements:

- *"I am going to experience more by living a life of courage."*
- *"Time is precious, I'm going to spend more of it with my family."*
- *"I am beautiful inside and will have my outside reflect this."*

2) *Specific goal – What*

This is your specific, value-based goal. What is valuable to you? What is your life missing? What do you want to be doing that so far you've only dreamed about? What are your unspoken passions?

Write your goal in the form of the positive rather than the negative. This allows you to work toward something rather than run away from something. Establish goals based on *"I want"* instead of *"I don't want."* *"I want to spend more time with my family"* rather than *"I don't want to spend as much time at work."* *"I want to travel more"* rather than *"I don't travel enough."*

Visualize the specific goal. For example, if you want a new home, visualize the house. Walk through it and around it. Feel it. The more detailed the better. "A new home" is insufficient to complete this WHAT component. "A 3,000 square foot Tudor house with 3 bedrooms, 2 to 3 baths, a back yard with at least 1 acre, and a view of the lake" is a more complete description of a goal. The more details you provide in your description, the more information you give to your subconscious mind. This results in a greater ability to clarify your purpose, set up your dominoes, and take inspired action.

How high should I set my goals? Set your goals high but not out of reach. Remember: optimistic and realistic. Have faith in your ability to conquer and succeed. Have faith in your ability to achieve greatness, because you can.

Measurable goals help provide you with more details to visualize and a greater sense of accomplishment when those objectives have been reached … and they will be reached!

3) When

With vision boards, you should never mention timelines because it could lead to disappointment, negativity, and no goal achievement. Further, you can't hold the universe to any timeline. On the contrary, when creating an Action Board, the "when" you are going to complete this goal is an important component and critical to being specific about your intention. *Not* setting a deadline and a timeline is one of the greatest reasons for people *not* achieving or even working toward their goals.

Goal setting research conclusively shows that, to be most effective, a goal must possess a clear starting time or date so that you identify when to begin working toward your goal and a well-defined completion time or date so you can definitively establish in your mind that this is a real goal with a real timeline. Giving your goal a deadline and publishing your due date on your Action Board helps push you to work harder to adhere to your own timeline.

One effective technique to incorporate when establishing your "when" is to divide your final goal into smaller, bite-sized pieces with specific dates or timelines for each of the bites. Consider breaking up your timeline into daily, weekly, or even monthly mini-goals. As in setting any of your goals, make your timeline optimistic (challenge yourself) but also realistic.

The "when" section of the Action Board is one of the most challenging. It's challenging because it's critical. Establishing a timeline is motivating and energizing, aligning all of the forces necessary either within your subconscious or within the universe.

4) *Motivators*

What is motivating you? Why do you care? Why is this goal important to you? Do you really care that much if it gets completed? We all have had goals that we gave up on. What makes this one so special?

Motivators are your driving forces that keep you going when things get tough. They give you a boost, an uplifting shot of energy when we start to get goal-fatigue. Motivators are Red Bull for the soul. They are literary or pictorial representations of your deep-seated inspirations. Motivators are typically phrases or pictures that are derived from your values and principles and, as such, they speak to you from a valuable place.

You began this journey by picking a goal, not at random, but because it meant something important to you. You did that by basing your goal on some core principle or value that you hold dear to your heart. Your *Motivators* are a direct reflection of the values that brought you to this goal. Goals that you view as crucial to who you need to become will be worth going through hell and back for, in order to make them happen. This will be your greatest motivational factor and driving force in the entire Action Board!

5) Commitments

The commitment component represents specific action steps that you plan on taking to achieve your goal. How exactly are you dedicated to make this happen? Every successful business needs a business plan. This is a process plan, a how-to description.

Without commitments, there are only hopes and dreams. You have written out your goal in a very specific fashion; the commitment section is where you further detail what *you* plan to do to realize this goal. To accomplish any goal, you need to be committed to it. It is important to realize that each of these commitments is also a Domino in your Action Board.

Some examples of commitments:
- I will cook at home at least three dinners per week.
- I will walk for 20 minutes at least six days per week.
- I will write my book for 20 minutes per day.

- I will not go to fast food restaurants more than once a week.

Commitment and engagement with work and relationships is what separates resilient, successful workers and spouses from unemployed and divorced people. When you are committed, you will cross the ocean for just one kiss; finish the marathon despite intense leg pain; tell the truth at work even though it may hurt your chances of promotion.

6) Challenges

While problems are debilitating and situations or issues are to be avoided, challenges may be empowering. How will you rise to the challenge?

In contrast to vision boards and the law of attraction, which view the topic of challenges as negatives to be avoided, delineating potential challenges should be regarded as a positive. Challenges help you plan for a variety of possibilities and may act as beneficial experiences for learning and growing; increasing the chance that pre-defined obstacles will become opportunities, rather than problems that will deter you from achieving your dreams.

When you challenge yourself, you go beyond who you think you are to reveal who you can be. Every challenge contains a blessing in disguise. Make a realistic list of challenges and obstacles that you are likely to face along your journey. Do this with a positive attitude and start to contemplate how you will rise to face these challenges. In addition to visualizing the process of how you will complete your goal, also envision how you will overcome your obstacles and what you will do to continue pursuit of your goal.

7) Strengths

You have talents. There are some general talents and strengths that will help you achieve most goals such as perseverance, determination, resilience, fortitude, and passion. There are other talents that you possess such as spirituality, religiosity, love of wisdom, communication, humor, athleticism, etc. that will be more beneficial for specific types of goals.

Using the DIVINE visualization process, envision what it will take to move from where you are now to where you want to be. What kind of person will it take to accomplish this goal? Decide which talents would best suit this journey and accomplish this task.

Which of these talents do you possess? You can also approach this from another direction. Do a self-assessment of your strengths. Try to come up with your top 5 to 10 strengths and envision how you may apply them to this particular goal. This may involve some 'out-of-the-box' thinking. The process of acknowledging and assessing your top personal strengths is enlightening and empowering. This exercise will inspire and embolden you to achieve more goals in the future.

8) Reinforcements

In addition to your talents and strengths, you have other resources that will be beneficial to your successful achievement of this goal. Resources may include finances you may need to make purchases, or other material objects that will be useful to accomplish this task. Go through your inventory of what special items you currently have that may come in useful while on your journey.

You may use DIVINE visualization to bring a clearer

understanding of things you may need to get started and items that may help you drive this process to completion. View yourself as commander of your army or conductor of your orchestra. It is not only *things* that serve as resources; important people in your life can also play important roles. We are part of a global community of goal achievers, all of us playing an active role in helping each other.

You have friends, family, coworkers, and neighbors who may be able to assist you in completing this goal. Further, you may have clergy—a pastor, priest, or rabbi—or perhaps a coach or mentor whose opinions you trust. These people may serve to be a great source of inspiration, information, or possibly even perspiration.

Acknowledging your reinforcements allows you to continually show gratitude to the people, and for the possessions, in your life.

9) Action

You will note that, in addition to being a component of the Action Board, "Inspired Action" is also one of the Key to Achieve Principles. What makes this so important as to command repeating? The answer is that without action, your dreams will remain wishes. Action is what moves the vision board into the next century of goal-achievement tools.

The vision board focuses on outcome visualization and the proper way to *set goals*. The Action Board focuses on process visualization and the proper way to *achieve goals*. There is debate among vision board enthusiasts about whether it is necessary to look at your vision board every day, or if the act of simply creating the board is enough to set the universe in motion. This motion attracts you to those things, or goals, you want. In contrast, in terms of the

Action Board, you should look at your board and visualize *what you will do* each day that you want to move forward on your goal. Taking just a few minutes to focus on your board will firmly reestablish your intention and put you in a much better mental place to visualize the process—how you will take action. Every day that you say to yourself you want this goal to be accomplished, take some degree of inspired action to make it happen! When you feel that some kind of goal-directed action is appropriate, that action step will be inspired. In fact, all action steps you now perform will be inspired and energized.

10. Dominations

When you integrate the Key to Achieve principles of Dominoes and Celebrations, you get the component of Dominations. What does it mean to Dominate? Domination is the process of celebrating the accomplishment of knocking down one of your dominoes. As you recall, dominoes are all of the commitments you have planned to make, all of your timeline goals, and all of your challenges.

The fact that all of these different components represent dominoes provides you with the opportunity to frequently enjoy mini-celebrations. If it sounds like you will be dominating too often, this is not the case. Yes, you may be dominating your goal several times per day, but this is not too often. Every time you climb up the flight of stairs at work, every time you decide not to go to McDonald's on the way home, every time you cook a healthy meal at home or don't overeat is another Domino is being knocked over.

The more often you celebrate your dominations, the more empowered, energized, and inspired you will be to pursue your goal with enthusiasm and passion. In addition to improving your motivation and self-esteem, more Dominations lead to greater satisfaction with life and overall well-being.

22

Conclusion

Vision boards are goal setting tools that have gained popularity over the past decade. They are a tangible representation of your dreams and wishes for the future; what you want to be, have, or do. Vision boards come in a variety of shapes and sizes. Depending on whose vision board system you are following, vision boards may also include some kind of motivational concept. The one thing that all vision boards have in common is the belief in and incorporation of the law of attraction. This is the foundation by which vision boards derive their method of outcome visualization.

The law of attraction, which began in the New Thought Movement in the late 1800s, is described as a universal law dictating, "Like *always* attracts like." This simple phrase means that what you put into the universe you will *always* get back. The basis for this law is metaphysical pseudoscience, half truths, and false suppositions. Every thought you have leaves your brain, and travels through the universal ether to create impressions in Formless stuff, manifesting the product of which you are thinking. The law of attraction has become a mystical deity. Yet this is not so. In reality, it is an unfounded, scientific theory.

The negative consequences of a belief in the law if attraction are not appreciated by many vision board proponents. Accepting the law of attraction necessitates that you: 1) *Always* avoid negatives. This includes not having empathy, avoiding any career in a helping or healing field, and not participating in any support groups. 2) Blame yourself for any goal not achieved. 3) Blame all victims for their plight. 4) Focus on the future and become mindless about the present. 5) Hope for the unrealistic possibility of reaching perfection. 6) Limit yourself to a less successful mode of visualization.

Even while you ask for and feel and think and want something with all your heart, if you have one little subconscious action that contradicts your thoughts, feelings, words, and other actions, you will foil the whole plan. The universe places a greater weight on negative indications and nothing happens independent of your thoughts.

The other universal law that we may compare to the law of attraction is the law of gravity. There are no books on how to best invoke the law of gravity. When you throw something into the air, it will fall down. Period! You don't need books, manuals, or instructions on how best to make things fall. The fact that there are no exceptions to the law of gravity makes it a universal law. I can use the law of gravity to predict exactly what will happen when I throw something into the air. In contrast, the law of attraction cannot be used to predict anything.

In addition to the law of attraction, there exist vision boards incorporating principles and concepts that would otherwise be quite beneficial for accomplishing goals. However, having a basis of the law of attraction precludes you from fully utilizing these other concepts. For example, while you are envisioning that you are living in the perfect future, you will be unable to plan, conceive of any challenges, or take any kind of action. You could do these things, but it would be a half-hearted attempt if you really believed that you had already attained your goal. To bring your thoughts, feeling, words, actions, and behaviors in line with your intentions and beliefs, you cannot truly visualize you are living a perfect future now and also go about your daily life trying to pursue that same goal. You will also not be able to fully enjoy the NOW, when you are living as if it is the perfect future. At some point, you have to return to reality!

With all of the evidence that there is no law of attraction, why not *"throw away your vision board"*? Why would you not want to give up a law stating that victims of rape, child abuse, spousal abuse, terrorist attacks, natural disasters, the holocaust, and slavery are all to blame for their difficulties? Many who believe in the law of attraction are infatuated with mysticism. Believing in mystical phenomena is exciting. It gives us hope and fulfills a spiritual need. We like to believe in holistic and alternative medicine, spirits, and unexplained miracles, occurrences, and the occult. However, when evidence becomes available that disproves and demystifies the phenomena, it is no longer healthy to continue your belief. It's great to dream, pray, trust, and believe that the law of attraction exists and hope that one day evidence will prove it. But continuing to believe despite overwhelming evidence against is not in your best interest.

Another reason that some are hesitant to give up belief in mystical phenomena is a confidence in the validity of serendipitous evidence. They point to the hundreds of times that vision boards have been successful and neglect the tens of millions of times that they have not. For example: After the presidential election, 50 psychics come forward to brag that they had successfully predicted who would win. This sounds very impressive. They must be really talented. Let's look at the evidence. Looking at their history, we find their average rate of predicting the winner in presidential elections over the past 10 years is 35%. They are wrong 65% of the time. This is worse than if they were to just draw names out of a hat. Are you still impressed?

Why does it appear that there are quite a few people who are successful at vision boards? There are two reasons. *First*, there is the placebo effect. This is a powerful, mind-altering phenomenon, where we experience physiological, psychological, and even genetic alterations due to inactive substances. In other words, we hope and expect it to work so much that it actually does, despite the fact that it is inert. The second reason is that there is a clear self-selection bias. Of those who make up vision boards, some will be successful. Just as of those who rub a rabbit's foot and throw a penny in a fountain, some will be successful. Of those who were unsuccessful, it is rare to hear from them. What would they have to brag about? Not being successful just means that you did it wrong anyway. Of the remaining few who were successful, these conquests are readily reported. This biases our data to make it look like a high rate of return. When, in fact, as John Assaraf has stated in his *Complete Vision Board Kit* book, the actual success rate is about **0.1%!**

There are those who concede, "Okay, you're right, I don't believe in *all* of the law of attraction." There are only four words in the law: "Like always attracts like." It's critical to appreciate that if you want to revise it by eliminating the word *"always"* then it is no longer a universal law. Now we're getting somewhere!

I have limited my analyses and critiques of the law of attraction to reasoning and scientific information. However, the responses that I have received from law of attraction devotees are often personal, derogatory, and emotional. Here is one such reaction: "The author [me] ... obviously a pessimistic, underachieving human being who is perhaps one of those 'energy vampires' we hear about." These responses do not address any of the scientific evidence; they merely state negative assumptions about my personality. Ironically, the negative emotions that they are expressing are contrary to the law of attraction and had there been such a law, would have prevented them from achieving their goals. For the record, in terms of being an underachiever, I have achieved, received, and accomplished more awards, certificates, diplomas, black belts, degrees, goals, and bucket-list items than most. I am financially secure and live an incredibly fulfilling and amazing life—all without any consideration to or invoking any fictitious laws.

What's the solution? *Throw away your vision board* and build an Action Board. The Action Board is not just a goal setting tool, it is a goal-achieving tool based on proven and powerful Key to Achieve principles derived from the latest mind-brain science research. The Action Board is not founded on feel good methodologies. Dominating your life is not difficult when you understand how to re-wire your mind, re-train your brain, and take inspired action.

The 'secret' is that there is no secret. God or the universe may help you attain your goals, but there is no guarantee. There is no *always*. The preponderance of books on the law of attraction exists because it is *not* a universal law that always delivers. Proponents are eager to sell you their special 'all access' to the law of attraction. They've found the right combination to open the door to the law of success and if that doesn't work they also sell snake-charming oil...

One of the Key to Achieve principles incorporated into the Action Board is the **Principle of Attraction.** This states, "Like *tends* to attract like." Positive thoughts, feelings, words, and actions *tend* to attract positive consequences and positive results. This is based on positive psychology and mind-brain science of re-training your brain's focus center, the reticular activating system (RAS). The truth is *ninety percent* of what you love about the law of attraction still applies to the principle of attraction, for example, the focus on positivity, what you put in is what you usually get out, practice gratitude, etc. Eliminating that last ten percent of the law of attraction that is not included in the principle of attraction (the universe always gives it to you) is empowering, enlightening, and liberating.

The Action Board helps you align your thoughts and your value-based goals. You create an inspired plan and take inspired action. It is your personal assistant and action planner. The Action Board pumps you up with daily, directed motivation and step-by-step tasks for achieving your objectives. The Action Board can be used for any type of goal, including obtaining luxury items, enhancing relationships, improving your business, advancing your career, stopping addictions or unhealthy habits, improving your parenting skills, reshaping your body, and more. Another great benefit of the Action Board is the principle of dominoes. We each set up our own personal journey and each task and challenge is a mini-goal or domino. This is a principle that goes hand-in-hand with the principle of Mindfulness; a conscious awareness and appreciation of the power of now. Inherent in this concept is that our dominoes are not set in stone. We can move them as we see fit based on external events or internal biofeedback. We alone are responsible for setting up our dominoes. Life is full of choices, full of 'get to's and 'want to's not 'got to's and 'have to's. The Domino principle also allows us to consider challenges, contemplate how we will rise to the challenge and then knock over our dominoes.

Every domino knocked over is DOMINATION. The Action Board is based on an action-oriented framework that tracks your progress with every domination. Through the Action Board, you will first establish your goals based on your deep-seated, core principles and values. This process energizes your goals and transforms them from wants to needs. We dream about where we want to go and have no map or idea of how to get there. You may have been told, "Let the universe deal with the 'how'." Well, you're still waiting... Time to Throw Away Your Vision Board! Time to get yourself a goal map—an Action Board.

How can I be so sure that the Action Board works? It is based on proven, ground-breaking mind-brain research of the best methods to achieve goals, the most effective ways to visualize, and the newest findings in positive psychology. I know it works because everyone who has accomplished their goals has done it through these Key to Achieve principles, whether or not they knew they were using them. Yes, that even includes the vision board experts who went outside of the law of attraction to establish value-based goals, set up plans, and take inspired action. They, not the universe, created their destiny.

They donated to charities, built businesses using business plans, visualized processes, and marketed their services to others in need.

Successful individuals are no different from you. They don't have special powers or better abilities to invoke mystical laws. You are just as capable of incredible accomplishments and you will, when you start building an inspired action plan. Taking action without direction can be a waste of time, effort, and energy. The direction is guided by the process of DIVINE visualization. Envision the future, the here and now, and then make the connection. This technique takes advantage of your brain's ability to focus (directing your RAS) and optimizes the connection of your conscious and subconscious minds. Through the Key to Achieve principles and DIVINE visualization, the Action Board boosts this connection and energizes your subconscious mind to help you transform these positive, life-changing messages into your reality.

The Action Board is a goal-achieving tool. It is not a book, a motivational system, or self-help mumbo jumbo. The Action Board is the direct result of mind-brain scientific research, verified with true world successes. The results are real, proven and fast. The Action Board allows you to finally start living the life you've only dreamed of. IT WORKS! You can benefit from this system as soon as you Throw Away Your Vision Board and start constructing your ACTION BOARD!

References:

Chapter 1

1) Joyce Schwarz: *The Vision Board*. Harper Design, 2009.
2) Ralph Waldo Emerson: *The American Scholar*. Oration delivered to the Phi Beta Kappa Society at Cambridge. 1837.
3) William James: *What is an Emotion?* Mind, ix. 189, 1884.
4) Emma Curtis Hopkins: *Class lessons,* 1888, Wise Woman Press, 2006.
5) Prentice Mulford: *Thoughts are Things*, 1889. Martino Fine Books, 2011.
6) James Allen: *As a Man Thinketh*, 1902, Soho Books, 2011.
7) Troward T: *The Edinburgh Lectures on Mental Science*, 1904.
8) William Walker Atkinson: *Thought-Force in Business and Everyday Life*, 1900.
9) William Walker Atkinson: *Thought Vibration or the Law of Attraction.* Advanced Thought Publishing, 1906.
10) William Walker Atkinson: *Dynamic Thought, or the Law of Vibrant Energy*. Segnogram Publishing, 1906.
11) Bruce MacLelland, *Prosperity Through Thought Force,* Elizabeth Towne, Nautilus Magazine, 1907.
12) Wallace Wattles: *The Science of Getting Rich. The Science of Being Well, The Science of Being Great.* The Elizabeth Towne Co. 1910. Cosimo Classics, 2010.
13) Napoleon Hill: *The Law of Success in Sixteen Lessons.* Tribecca Books, 1928. Wilder Productions, 2011.
14) Napoleon Hill: *Think and Grow Rich.* 1936.
15) Napoleon Hill and W. Clement Stone: *Success Through a Positive Mental Attitude*. Prentice Hall, 1960.
16) Earl Nightingale: *The Strangest Secret.* Recorded 1959. Merchant

Books, 2013.
17) W. Clement Stone: *The Success System that Never Fails.* Simon & Schuster, 1962.
18) Shakti Gawain: *Creative Visualization.* 1978. New World Library, 2002.
19) Bob Proctor: *You are Born Rich. Now You Can Discover and Develop Those Riches.* McCrary Publications, 1984.
20) Rhonda Byrne: *The Secret.* Atria Books. 2006.
21) Esther and Jerry Hicks: *The Law of Attraction: The Basics of the Teachings of Abraham.* Hay House, 2006.
22) John Assaraf: *The Vision Board Book*, Atria Books, 2008.
23) Jack Canfield and DD Watkins: *Key to Living the Law of Attraction.* Health Comm Inc., 2007.
24) Meera Lester: *365 Ways to Live the Law of Attraction.* Adams Media, 2009.
25) Robert Worstell:. *Secrets to the Law of Attraction.* Worstell Foundation, 2011.
26) Joe Vitale: *The Key: The Missing Secret for Attracting Anything You Want.* Wiley, 2007.
27) Joe Vitale: *The Attractor Factor: 5 easy steps for creating wealth from the inside out,* Wiley, 2008.

Chapter 2
1) Rhonda Byrne: *The Secret.* Atria Books. 2006.
2) John Assaraf: *The Vision Board Book*, Atria Books, 2008.
3) Marcia Layton Turner: *The Complete Idiot's Guide to Vision Boards.* Alpha, 2009.

Chapter 3
1) Rhonda Byrne: *The Secret.* Atria Books. 2006.

2) Michael Shermer: *Why People Believe Weird Things: Pseudoscience, Superstition, and Other Confusions of Our Time.* Holt Paperbacks, 2002.

Chapter 4

1) William Walker Atkinson: *Dynamic Thought, or the Law of Vibrant Energy.* Segnogram Publishing, 1906.

2) William Walker Atkinson: *Practical Mental Influence. Mental Vibrations, Psychic Influence, Personal Magnetism, Fascination, Psychic Self-Protection, etc.* Advanced Thought Publications Co. 1908.

3) R Shankar: *Principles of Quantum Mechanics.* Plenum Press, 2nd ed., 2008.

4) Brian R. Martin: *Particle Physics.* Oneworld Publications, 2011.

5) Alastair Rae: *Quantum Physics.* Oneworld Publications, 2005.

6) Norman Doidge: *The Brain that Changes Itself.* Penguin Books, 2007.

7) John B. Arden: *Rewire Your Brain: Think Your Way to a Better Life.* Wiley, 2010.

8) Jeffrey M. Schwartz: *The Mind and the Brain: Neuroplasticity and the Power of Mental Force.* ReaganBooks, 2003.

9) Mark F. Bear, Barry W. Connors, Michael A. Paradiso: *Neuroscience: Exploring the Brain.* Lippincott, Williams and Wilkins, 3rd ed., 2006.

10) Greg Kuhn: *Why Quantum Physicists Do Not Fail.* Create Space. 2012.

11) Pam Grout: *E2: Nine Do-It-Yourself Experiments That Prove Your Thoughts Create Your Reality.* Hay House, 2013.

12) Candace Pert: *Molecules of Emotion: Science Behind the Mind-Body Medicine.* Simon & Schuster, 1999.

13) Michael Shermer: *Why People Believe Weird Things: Pseudoscience, Superstition, and Other Confusions of Our Time.* Holt Paperbacks, 2002.

Chapter 5:

1) Pam Grout: *E2: Nine Do-It-Yourself Experiments That Prove Your Thoughts Create Your Reality*. Hay House, 2013.
2) Wallace Wattles: *The Science of Getting Rich*. The Elizabeth Towne Co. 1910. Cosimo Classics, 2010.
3) Esther and Jerry Hicks: *Money, and the Law of Attraction: Learning to Attract Wealth, Health, and Happiness*. Hay House, 2008.
4) Rhonda Byrne: *The Secret*. Atria Books. 2006.
5) Joe Vitale: *The Attractor Factor: 5 easy steps for creating wealth from the inside out*, Wiley, 2008.
6) Napoleon Hill: *Think and Grow Rich*. 1936.
7) Stephen Covey, A. Roger Merrill, Rebecca R. Merrill, *First Things First: To Live, to Love, to Learn, to Leave a Legacy*. New York: Simon and Schuster, 1994.

Chapter 6:

1) Genevieve Behrend: *Your Invisible Power*. Watchmaker Pub, 2013.
2) John Assaraf: *The Vision Board Book*. Atria Books, 2008.
3) Marcia Layton Turner: *The Complete Idiot's Guide to Vision Boards*. Alpha, 2009.

Chapter 7

1) William Walker Atkinson: *Thought Vibration or the Law of Attraction*. Advanced Thought Publishing, 1906.
2) Wallace Wattles: *The Science of Getting Rich. The Science of Being Well, The Science of Being Great*. The Elizabeth Towne Co. 1910. Cosimo Classics, 2010.
3) Prentice Mulford: *Thoughts are Things*, 1889. Martino Fine Books, 2011.
4) Napoleon Hill: *Think and Grow Rich*. 1936.

5) S Shane: *Sit down now and write that business plan.* Entrepreneur Journal online. Feb 1, 2012.

Chapter 8

1) Y Fried, LH Slowik: *Enriching goal-setting theory with time: an integrated approach.* Acad of Management Rev. 29, 2004.
2) Rhonda Byrne: *The Secret.* Atria Books. 2006.

Chapter 9

1) James Allen: *As a Man Thinketh*, 1902, Soho Books, 2011.
2) Wallace Wattles: *The Science of Getting Rich. The Science of Being Well, The Science of Being Great.* The Elizabeth Towne Co. 1910. Cosimo Classics, 2010.

Chapter 10

1) Stephen G. Post: *Altruism, Happiness, and Health: It's Good to Be Good.* Int J Behav Med. 12, 2005.
2) Stephen G. Post: *Altruism and Health: Perspectives from Empirical Research.* APA, Oxford Univ. Press. 2007.
3) Rhonda Byrne: *The Secret.* Atria Books. 2006.

Chapter 11

1) A Docherty: *Experience, functions, and benefits of a cancer support group.* Patient. Educ. Counc. 55, 2004.
2) A Rigsby, DM Gropper, SS Gropper: *Success of women in a worksite weight loss program: Does being part of a group help?* Eat Behav 10, 2009.

Chapter 12

1) Esther and Jerry Hicks: *The Law of Attraction: The Basics of the Teachings of Abraham.* Hay House, 2006.
2) Rhonda Byrne: *The Secret.* Atria Books. 2006.
3) Eckhart Tolle: *The Power of Now.* New World Library, 2004.

4) Pam Grout: *E2: Nine Do-It-Yourself Experiments That Prove Your Thoughts Create Your Reality.* Hay House, 2013.

5) G Oettingen, TA Wadden: *Expectation, fantasy, and weight loss: Is the impact of positive thinking always positive?* Cog Ther and Res, 15, 1991.

6) G Oettingen, D Mayer: *The motivating function of thinking about the future: Expectations versus fantasies.* J Pers & Soc Psych, 83, 2002.

7) DW Kearns, J Crossman: *Effects of a cognitive intervention package on the free throw performance of varsity basketball players during practice and competition.* Perceptual and Motor Skills, 75, 1992.

8) J Nelson, DR Czech, et al: *The effects of video and cognitive imagery on throwing performance of baseball pitchers:* The Sport J, 11, 2008.

9) RW Coelho, W deCampos, et al: *Imagery intervention in open and closed tennis motor skill performance.* Perceptual and Motor Skills, 105, 2007.

10) W Rodgers, C Hall, E Buckolz: *The effect of an imagery training program on imagery ability, imagery use, and figure skating performance.* J App Sport Psychol, 3, 1991.

11) Scott Swainston, Noah Gentner, et al: *The Effect of PETTLEP Imagery in a Pre- Shot Routine on Full Swing Golf Shot Accuracy: A Single Subject Design.* Int J Golf Science, 1, 2012.

12) RJ Rotella, B Gansneder, D Ojala, J Billing: *Cognitions and coping strategies of elite skiers: an exploratory study of young developing athletes. J. Sport Psychology* 2, 1980.

13) Lien Pham, Shelley Taylor: *From Thought to Action: Effects of Process-Versus Outcome-Based Mental Simulations on Performance.* J Person & Soc Psychology Bull. (25), 1999.

14) Shelley E. Taylor, Lien B. Pham, et al: *Harnessing the imagination:*

Mental simulation, self-regulation, and coping. Am Psychol, 53, 1998.

15) Ursula Debarnot, Emeline Clerget, Etienne Olivier: *Role of the primary motor cortex in the early boost in performance following mental imagery training.* PloS one 6, 2011.

16) Tori Rodriguez: *Mental imagery techniques help abuse victims.* Scientific American, June, 2012.

17) G Oettingen, D Mayer, et al: *Mental contrasting and expectancy-dependent goal commitment: The mediating role of energization.* Pers and Soc Psychol Bull, 35, 2009.

18) Joyce Schwarz: *The Vision Board.* Harper Design, 2009.

Chapter 13

1) Neville Goddard: *Feeling is the Secret.* Pacific Pub. Studio. 2010.
2) Greg Kuhn: *Why Quantum Physicists Do Not Fail.* Create Space. 2012.
3) Esther and Jerry Hicks: *The Law of Attraction: The Basics of the Teachings of Abraham.* Hay House, 2006.
4) Pam Grout: *E2: Nine Do-It-Yourself Experiments That Prove Your Thoughts Create Your Reality.* Hay House, 2013.
5) Stephen Covey: *The 7 Habits of Highly Effective People.* Franklin Covey, DC Books, 2005.
6) John Assaraf: *The Vision Board Book.* Atria Books, 2008.

Chapter 14

1) Greg Kuhn: *Why Quantum Physicists Do Not Fail.* Create Space. 2012.
2) James Allen: *As a Man Thinketh,* 1902, Soho Books, 2011.
3) Wallace Wattles: *The Science of Getting Rich. The Science of Being Well, The Science of Being Great.* The Elizabeth Towne Co. 1910. Cosimo Classics, 2010.
4) Esther Hicks as Abraham, San Diego, Feb 23, 2002.

Chapter 15

1) Tal Ben-Shahar: *The Pursuit of Perfect: How to Stop Chasing Perfection and Start Living a Richer, Happier Life.* McGraw-Hill, 2009.

2) A Kappes, G Oettingen, H Pak: *Mental Contrasting and the Self-Regulation of Responding to Negative Feedback.* Pers Soc Psychol Bull. 38, 2012.

3) A-K. Klesse, et al: *Repeated exposure to the thin ideal and implications for the self: two weight loss program studies.* Int J Marketing Res. 29, 2012.

4) G Oettingen, TA Wadden: *Expectation, fantasy, and weight loss: Is the impact of positive thinking always positive?* Cog. Ther & Res 15, 1991.

Chapter 16

1) I Kirsch, G Sapirstein: *Listening to Prozac but hearing placebo: A meta-analysis of antidepressant medication.* Prevention & Treatment, 1, 1998.

2) A Hróbjartsson, M Norup: *The use of placebo interventions in medical practice--a national questionnaire survey of Danish clinicians.* Eval & the Health Prof 26, 2003.

3) Romeo Vitelli: Exploring the Placebo Effect. Psychology Today online, Nov. 11, 2012.

4) P Petrovic, E Kalso, et al: *Placebo and opioid analgesia: Imaging a shared neuronal network.* Science, 295, 1737, 2002.

5) S Rajagopal: *The nocebo effect.* Found at http://priory.com/medicine/Nocebo.htm, 2007

6) John Assaraf: *The Vision Board Book.* Atria Books, 2008

Chapter 17

1) JJ Deeks, J Dinnes, R D'Amico et al: *Evaluating non-randomised*

intervention studies. Health Technology Assessment, 7, 2003.

2) John Assaraf: *The Vision Board Book.* Atria Books, 2008.
3) Wallace Wattles: *The Science of Getting Rich. The Science of Being Well, The Science of Being Great.* The Elizabeth Towne Co. 1910. Cosimo Classics, 2010.
4) Napoleon Hill: *Think and Grow Rich.* 1936.
5) Carl G. Jung: *Man & His Symbols.* Dell, 1968.
6) Michael Shermer: *Why People Believe Weird Things: Pseudoscience, Superstition, and Other Confusions of Our Time.* Holt Paperbacks, 2002.
7) Pam Grout: *E2: Nine Do-It-Yourself Experiments That Prove Your Thoughts Create Your Reality.* Hay House, 2013.

Chapter 18

1) John Assaraf: *The Vision Board Book.* Atria Books, 2008.
2) Neville Goddard: *Feeling is the Secret. Ideas that Shape the World.* Pacific Publishing Studio. 2010.
3) Alexander Janzer: *Manifesting: The Secret Behind the Law of Attraction.* CreateSpace, 2010.
4) Robert Collier: *The Secret of Ages.* Snowball Publishing, 2012.
5) Sonia M Miller: *The Attraction Distraction: Why the Law of Attraction Isn't Working for You and How to Get Results – FINALLY!* Alma Publishing, Inc., 2008.
6) Jack Canfield and DD Watkins: *Key to Living the Law of Attraction.* Health Communications Inc., 2007.
7) Meera Lester: *365 Ways to Live the Law of Attraction.* Adams Media, 2009.
8) Robert Worstell: *Secrets to the Law of Attraction.* Worstell Foundation, 2011.

9) Joe Vitale: *The Key: The Missing Secret for Attracting Anything You Want*. Wiley, 2007.

10) Joe Vitale: *The Attractor Factor: 5 easy steps for creating wealth from the inside out*. Wiley, 2008.

11) Joyce Schwarz: *The Vision Board*. Harper Design, 2009.

Chapter 19

1) John Assaraf: *The Vision Board Book*. Atria Books, 2008.

Chapter 20

1) Neil E Farber: *The Blame Game: The Complete Guide to Blaming. How to Play and How to Quit*. Bascom Hill Press, 2010.

2) Stephen Covey: *The 7 Habits of Highly Effective People*. Franklin Covey, DC Books, 2005.

3) Stephen Covey, A. Roger Merrill, Rebecca R. Merrill, *First Things First: To Live, to Love, to Learn, to Leave a Legacy*. New York: Simon and Schuster, 1994

4) Eckhart Tolle: *The Power of Now*. New World Library, 2004.

5) Pham LB, Taylor SE: *From Thought to Action: Effects of Process-Versus Outcome-Based Mental Simulations on Performance*. Pers Soc Psychol Bull. 25, 1999.

6) Daniel J Siegel: *Mindfulness training and neural integration: differentiation of distinct streams of awareness and the cultivation of well-being*. Social Cognitive and Affect. Neuroscience. (2), 2007.

7) Tal Ben Shahar: *Happier: Learn the Secrets to Daily Joy and Lasting Fulfillment*. McGraw-Hill, 2007.

8) Ed Diener, Robert Biswas-Diener: *Happiness: Unlocking the Mysteries of Psychological Wealth*. Wiley-Blackwell, 2008.

9) Barbara Fredrickson: *Positivity*: Harmony, 2009

10) Christopher Peterson: *A Primer in Positive Psychology*. Oxford

University Press, 2006.

11) Neil E Farber: *Making Lemonade: 101 Recipes to Convert Negatives into Positives*. Dynamic Publishing Group, 2012.

12) Neil E Farber: *8 Key Principles to Succeed*. Psychology Today.com, Sept, 2013.

13) Neil E Farber: *Dominoes vs Rainbows. Practical Goal Setting*. PsychologyToday.com, Dec 11, 2011.

14) Neil E Farber: *The Domino Effect: A Mindfully Positive Path to Goal-Setting*. PsychologyToday.com, Feb 7, 2012.

15) G Oettingen, TA Wadden: *Expectation, fantasy, and weight loss: Is the impact of positive thinking always positive?* Cog Ther and Res, 15, 1991.

16) G Oettingen, D Mayer: *The motivating function of thinking about the future: Expectations versus fantasies*. J Pers and Soc Psych, 83, 2002.

17) Lien Pham, Shelley Taylor: *From Thought to Action: Effects of Process-Versus Outcome-Based Mental Simulations on Performance*. J Person & Soc Psychology Bull. (25), 1999.

18) Shelley E Taylor, Lien B Pham, et al: *Harnessing the imagination: Mental simulation, self-regulation, and coping*. Am Psychol, 53, 1998.

19) G Oettingen, D Mayer, et al: *Mental contrasting and expectancy-dependent goal commitment: The mediating role of energization*. Pers and Soc Psychol Bull, 35, 2009.

20) RJ Rotella, B Gansneder, D Ojala, J Billing: *Cognitions and coping strategies of elite skiers: an exploratory study of young developing athletes*. J. Sport Psychology 2, 1980.

Index

accountability 92, 132, 134, 135
action board ii, iii, ix, 16, 86, 106, 118, 128-137, 141, 144-149, 152, 153, 159-162
Allen, James 5, 68, 95
alpha waves 33
antidepressant 105
anger cells 35-36
April Fool's 114
archetypes 86
apophenia 111, 112, 118
Assaraf, John ix, 14, 17, 18, 55, 75, 79, 90, 92, 106, 109, 110, 112, 123, 130, 158
Atkinson, William 6, 7, 25, 59
Bathtubs 114
Beck, Martha 109
Beckwith, Michael Bernard 95, 100, 108
Behrend, Genevieve 53
Bible 2, 8
blame vii, 89, 92, 94, 98, 121, 136, 140, 156, 157
Buddhism 3
Byrne, Rhonda vii, 9, 13, 14, 53, 54, 60-63, 65, 69, 71, 80, 81, 84, 89, 90, 93, 94, 99, 122

Canfield, Jack 15, 38, 53, 61, 63, 69, 90, 92, 100, 123
Cardiff Giant 113
challenges 17, 23, 61, 63, 64, 67-69, 82, 83, 97, 124, 134, 135, 141, 148, 150, 153, 157, 160, 161
college students 82, 83, 88, 102,
commitments 149, 150, 153
Cottingley Fairies 114
Covey, Steven 48, 92, 136
dominator 146
dominoes 134, 141, 147, 149, 153, 160, 161
Dooley, Mike 61, 81
dreams ix, 16, 17, 19, 24, 46, 47, 55, 56, 58, 59, 61, 64, 66, 69, 79, 83, 86, 87, 89, 92, 99, 101, 104, 109, 116, 130, 131, 141, 145, 149, 150, 152, 155, 157, 161
electric 9, 26, 27, 30, 32, 34-36, 42, 118, 137
electroencephalogram 34, 36, 37
electron 28, 30, 39, 42, 43
Emerson, Ralph Waldo 4
energy vi, vii, 7, 8, 11, 12, 15, 18, 22, 26-28, 30-43, 59, 60, 72, 85, 88, 89, 116-120, 124, 132, 133,

136, 148, 159, 162
ether 10, 14, 29, 34, 38, 39, 117, 120, 126, 135, 155
fluid 10, 30, 33, 36, 37, 39
focus v, x, 9, 12, 13-15, 17-19, 35, 41, 46, 48, 49, 55-57, 59, 64, 71, 79, 81, 86-88, 90, 91, 108, 109, 111, 112, 132-134, 136, 137, 142-145, 152, 153, 156, 160, 162
formless stuff 9, 24, 40, 41, 56, 120, 155
Gawain, Shakti 12
Gratitude 14, 19, 21, 110, 131, 134, 138, 152, 160
Grout, Pam 42. 46, 81, 91, 113, 116
Haanel, Charles 53, 100
healing 22, 84, 85, 156
Hicks,
    Abraham 14, 97
    Esther 13, 14, 23, 54, 60, 62, 68, 79, 81, 90, 91, 93-98, 100
    Jerry 13,14, 97
Hill, Napolean 10-13, 39, 55, 59, 60, 63, 66, 92, 95, 96, 110
Hopkins, Emma Curtis 5
illness 10, 14, 71, 72, 75, 94, 96, 98, 120, 121, 133, 139, 140
immersive stimulation 88
James, William 4
jobs 75, 82, 83, 139
Jones, Dr. Steve 65, 66
Lien Pham 83
Loch Ness Monster 115
MacLelland, Bruce 7-9
mastermind 39
mental cleansing 87
metaphysics /metaphysical viii, 4, 6, 15, 25, 117, 118, 130, 155
mind-brain viii, ix, 88, 130, 159-162
mindful 3, 22, 41, 81, 85, 122, 134, 136, 137, 141, 161
mirror neurons 36, 38
motivators 148, 149
Mulford, Prentice 5, 59
Naked Stranger 114
New Thought v, 3-7, 9, 59, 66, 69, 108, 155, 159
Nichols, Lisa 69, 80, 90, 100
Nightingale, Earl 11, 12
optimism 8, 131, 137, 139-141
outcome 40, 65, 78, 79, 81-88, 91, 99, 100, 105, 107, 112, 132, 133, 135-137, 141, 142, 152, 155

overweight 49, 71, 73, 76, 94
performance 83, 101
Pert Candace 44
photons 30
Pillay, Srini 55
Piltdown man 113
placebo 104-107, 158
plans 46, 55, 57, 59-63, 66, 67, 69, 85, 93, 112, 119, 120, 122, 124, 131, 133, 150, 156, 160-162
positivity 15, 21, 79, 110, 128, 132, 133, 137, 138, 160
poverty 63, 70, 71, 74, 95, 96, 98, 140
Principle of Attraction 134, 138-140, 144, 160
process v, 3, 16, 19, 23, 61, 64, 81-88, 97, 104, 106, 113, 125, 131-134, 137, 138, 141-144, 149-153, 161, 162
Proctor, Bob 12, 13, 40, 41, 60, 63, 90, 95
purpose 18, 21, 25, 46, 48-50, 68, 78, 99, 136, 147
psychodynamics 87
quantum field theory 40-43
quantum physics (mechanics) 30, 40, 42, 43, 117
Ray, James 100
reinforcements 112, 113, 151, 152
reticular activating system (RAS) 143, 160, 162
Roman 3
Sapirstein Guy 105
Schwarz, Joyce vi, 2, 14, 55, 75, 79, 85-87
self-blame 89, 92, 93, 120, 121, 132, 134, 136, 139, 156
Shermer, Michael 22, 45
sound 10, 29-31, 33, 46, 122
sport 83
Spurling, Christina 115
Stone, Clement W 12
strengths 47, 67, 83, 86, 87, 132, 137, 141, 142, 151
support groups 75, 76, 121, 122, 156
symbology 86
Taylor, Shelley 83
The Secret v, vii, 5, 6, 9, 11, 13-19, 22-24, 47, 52, 55, 57, 60, 62, 66, 70, 71, 74, 76, 79, 92, 95, 96, 100, 108, 110, 122, 123, 135

thought waves 24, 30, 34, 36, 39
timeline 64-66, 69, 147, 148, 153
Troward, Thomas 6
universal law 24, 28, 42, 75, 89, 109, 118-120, 127, 139, 155, 156, 158, 159
values ix, 14, 18, 48-50, 124, 132-134, 136, 141, 144-146, 149, 160, 161
victim 76, 84, 87, 88, 94, 98, 138, 140, 156, 157
vibration 7, 8, 10, 13, 18, 19, 26, 28-32, 35, 39, 41, 91, 97, 100, 117, 126
visualize v, vii, ix, 3, 12, 16, 17, 19-21, 23, 24, 41, 46, 50-53, 55, 57, 59, 62, 65, 69, 78, 79, 81-88, 92, 99, 106, 107, 122, 125-127, 131-133, 136, 137, 142-145, 147, 150, 152, 153, 161, 162, 155-157
   DIVINE 88, 132-134, 141-144, 147, 151, 162
Vitale, Joe viii, 15, 22, 53, 54, 60, 61, 63, 65, 69, 80, 84, 90, 138
War of the Worlds 114
Wattles, Wallace 9, 10, 13, 52,
59, 68, 70, 73, 96, 97, 99, 110
Wilson, Robert 115
Winfrey, Oprah vi, 13, 109
word association 86
Zigler, Zig 144

Neil E. Farber, MD, PhD

QUICK ORDER FORM:

Throw Away Your Vision Board

Email orders: neil@NeilFarber.com

Please send the following books. I understand that I may return any of them for a full refund—for any reason.

- [ ] The Blame Game
- [ ] Making Lemonade
- [ ] The No Blaming Zone
- [ ] The Financial Industry's Guide to the No Blaming Zone
- [ ] Throw Away Your Vision Board

Please send more free information on:

- [ ] Coaching [ ] Speaking/Seminars [ ] Consulting

Name: _____

Address: _____

City:_____ State: _____ Zip:_____

Telephone: _____

Email address: _____

Sales tax: Please add 5.6% for products shipped to Wisconsin addresses.

Shipping by air:

U.S. $4.50 for first book and $2.00 for each additional book.
International: $9.50 for first book, $5.00 for each additional book.

Neil E. Farber, MD, PhD

About the Author

Neil Farber received his Bachelor of Science degree with Honors in Psychology and dual doctorate degrees in Research and Medicine. He is a Psychology Professor and recently retired Pediatric Anesthesiologist and Associate Professor of Pediatrics, Pharmacology & Toxicology and Anesthesiology. Dr. Farber has been inducted into many Honor Societies and Martial Arts Hall of Fame, received numerous research and clinical awards and recognized as a "Top Doctor," "Leader in Healthcare" and "Doctor of Excellence." He is a member of the International Positive Psychology Association, writes for *Psychology Today*'s Happiness section and has over 150 publications. Dr. Farber is known as "The Rock Doc" as he has been the personal physician of many celebrities including Billy Joel, Elton John, Bob Dylan, Bette Midler, Kiss, Brittney Spears, Katy Perry and The Rolling Stones. Dr. Farber is the Chief Wellness Officer for the Dynamic Health & Wellness Institute, a Certified Life Coach, Personal Trainer and Martial Arts Grandmaster. He enjoys spending time with his fabulous family and volunteers on 3rd world medical missions, to which a portion of his book proceeds are donated. He has a blessed life, no part of which is attributed to a law of attraction.

Contact: Neil@NeilFarber.com
Facebook: Facebook/TheActionBoard   **Twitter**: @neilfarber
Check out www.NeilFarber.com

Printed in Great Britain
by Amazon